T0247696

PRAISE FOR
TÍAS AND PRIMAS

"In this collection of cuentos, Prisca Dorcas Mojica Rodríguez advances her commitment to 'democratize knowledge' by bringing her own 'book smart' insights home to la familia latina. Mojica Rodríguez paints portraits that resonate for Latinas and immigrant women who suffer the deep and daily pangs of patriarchy without a clear name for it. This book provides the names and counsels with compassionate knowing. A warrior against vergüenza, Mojica Rodríguez strives for a feminist and liberated latinidad. Her story may not be all of our stories, but we will recognize our relations, perhaps even our ancestors, in this telling. It is a significant gift."

—Cherríe Moraga, author of *Native Country of the Heart*

"Within these pages, I found my abuela, my tías, and my primas—laughing, crying, and nodding alongside me. This book is a gift of understanding and loving one's family, even when our families are complicated and painful. It's a beautiful reminder of the power of storytelling and the profound connection of kinship."

—Paola Mendoza, author, organizer, and filmmaker

"Part memoir, part sociology, part family reunion—Mojica Rodríguez shows her revolutionary vision once again: By honoring the tías and primas of her past and present, Mojica Rodríguez is cultivating a new path forward. This is a book that will save lives."

—José Olivarez, author of *Promises of Gold*

"Once in a lifetime, a reader finds a book that answers questions they didn't even know they had. In *Tías and Primas*, Mojica Rodríguez lovingly brings the truth to the archetypes of women we are all raised by, thus giving context to what our mothers, aunts, cousins, and sisters have lived. The childless tía now becomes a woman with autonomy and power. The standoffish prima can understand why she hesitates to connect to other women in her family. This love letter to intergenerational relationships opens every window and door to one's heart, allowing the reader to see the women in their lives as complex beings who have overcome generations of trauma. *Tías and Primas* is a healing work of art, an urgent beckoning to one's own understanding."

—Yesika Salgado, author of *Corazón*

"Reading through the pages of *Tías and Primas* reminded me of my own upbringing: the lessons I learned and the ones I had to unlearn as an adult. Mojica Rodríguez illuminates the complexities of intergenerational trauma, navigating machismo, and domestic life among the women who shape us with tenderness and empathy, while penning a love letter to the fierce and the outcast women who sacrificed and fought so we could be liberated. This is an important read for any woman seeking to live life on her terms."

—Saraciea J. Fennell, editor and
contributor, *Wild Tongues Can't Be Tamed*

"A heartwarming ode to America's most overlooked heroines, Mojica Rodríguez's latest work is more than a book. It's a once-in-a-lifetime experience. Imagine a slumber party with all the wild women, dead or alive, who made you into the warrior that you are. *Tías and Primas* is just that: a soul-nourishing, sparkling experience full of magic and secrets. You'll emerge feeling seen, with newfound strength to fight the systems that seek to erase women like you."

—Jean Guerrero, author of
*Crux: A Daughter's Quest for
Her Border-Crossing Father*

"*Tías and Primas* is the family reunion you've always wanted, and one you can return to each time you open this beautiful book. Mojica Rodríguez is our loving guide, exploring and adoring the feminine archetypes we grew up with."

—Virgie Tovar, author of
You Have the Right to Remain Fat

"This book goes beyond the idea of tías and primas as solely familial. Even those of us with complicated family histories will find ourselves and the families that we have chosen for ourselves in these pages. Each tía and prima archetype is a person we know, a person we have been, or a person we wish to become. Each chapter culminates in the way any conversation with a loved one would—with loving guidance, invitations for self-reflection, and affirmations that feel like bendiciones. This book is the tía and prima we all need."

—Elisabet Velasquez, author of
When We Make It

"Mojica Rodríguez's powerful storytelling gives voice to emotions often suppressed for survival, but necessary if we are to become who we need to become. Offering moral wisdom through the lives of the women who raise us, Mojica Rodríguez not only beautifully weaves tales but contextualizes them in sociopolitical theory that indicts the systems that injure us and gently points the way back to who we desire to be."

—Dr. Courtney Bryant, author of *Erotic Defiance*

"*Tías and Primas* is an artful examination of the women, and systems, that shape our lives. Through an expansive blend of genres, from memoir to social theory, Mojica Rodríguez crafts a compassionate guide for better understanding our loved ones, chosen and biological. This book traverses many realms—from ghosts to respectability politics to MLMs—without ever losing sight of the rich inner lives of the tías and primas at its core. Sharp-toothed and compassionate, Mojica Rodríguez exposes our societal shortcomings, while always insisting that better, healthier, and more equitable connections are possible. A book I will gift again and again."

—Ruben Reyes Jr., author of
There is a Rio Grande in Heaven

TÍAS AND PRIMAS

ON KNOWING
AND LOVING THE WOMEN
WHO RAISE US

PRISCA DORCAS MOJICA RODRÍGUEZ

Illustrations by Josie Del Castillo

SEAL PRESS

New York

Seal Press
Hachette Book Group
1290 Avenue of the Americas, New York, NY 10104
www.sealpress.com
@sealpress

Printed in the United States of America

First Edition: September 2024

Published by Seal Press, an imprint of Hachette Book Group, Inc. The Seal Press name and logo is a registered trademark of the Hachette Book Group.

The Hachette Speakers Bureau provides a wide range of authors for speaking events. To find out more, go to hachettespeakersbureau.com or email HachetteSpeakers@hbgusa.com.

Seal books may be purchased in bulk for business, educational, or promotional use. For more information, please contact your local bookseller or the Hachette Book Group Special Markets Department at special.markets@hbgusa.com.

The publisher is not responsible for websites (or their content) that are not owned by the publisher.

Illustrations by Josie Del Castillo.
Print book interior design by Bart Dawson.

Library of Congress Control Number: 2024003615

ISBNs: 9781541603950 (hardcover), 9781541603967 (ebook)

LSC-C

Printing 1, 2024

For the women who have found
true love among other women.

CONTENTS

INTRODUCTION

1

Chapter 1

LA MATRIARCH

15

Chapter 2

THE YOUNG TÍA

29

Chapter 3

LA PRIMA PERFECTA

41

Chapter 4

WIDOWED TÍA

55

Chapter 5

TU TÍA, LA LOCA

67

Chapter 6

THE TÍA WHO SEES FANTASMAS

79

Chapter 7

STREET-SMART PRIMA

93

Chapter 8
DIGNIFIED TÍA
107

Chapter 9
TÍA WHO LOVES PLANTS AND ANIMALS
119

Chapter 10
TU TÍA ESCANDALOSA
129

Chapter 11
PRIMA WHO DOESN'T LIKE OTHER WOMEN
141

Chapter 12
THE CHILDLESS TÍA
155

Chapter 13
THE "TE ESTÁS ENGORDANDO" TÍA
167

Chapter 14
BOOK-SMART PRIMA
179

Chapter 15
DIVORCED TÍA
193

Chapter 16
SECOND MOM TÍA
205

Chapter 17
WHATSAPP TÍA
219

Chapter 18
LA TÍA CUIR
231

Chapter 19
MLM TÍA
243

Chapter 20
YOUR "PRETTY" PRIMA
253

CONCLUSION
265

ACKNOWLEDGMENTS
271

NOTES
273

BIBLIOGRAPHY
285

INTRODUCTION

A FEW YEARS AGO, I ASKED MY MAMI ABOUT A TÍA I GREW UP WITH BUT seldom get to see. That year I was headed to the motherland after almost six years away, and I wanted to prepare myself for what and whom I was about to see again.

This woman I call a tía is not biologically related to me, but I hold her in high regard like I do my own family. She is my kin. When I inquired about this tía, my mami said, "She lives somewhere else now," her voice trailing off. And she kept saying things like that, answers that did not feel like answers. Answers that only gave way to more questions, and so I kept asking more. Maybe I should have caught on to the obvious discomfort mi mami was having with explicating all this to me, but I was relentless. Mi mami has consistently expressed distaste and discomfort when talking about this tía, and I had grown accustomed to it. I had become comfortable with pushing past her tone drenched with indirectness.

Eventually, what I gathered was that this tía was now openly queer and living with her partner. She had moved away from the city of Managua to the outskirts—either for her safety or to keep away from what people who knew her would say about her—is what I understood. This was what was implied, and I sat with it.

1

My initial feeling was one of elation for this tía. I felt warmth in my chest and arms, like when you take a sip of something hot on a treacherously cold day outdoors. The feeling engulfed me. Then it was followed by scorn for mi mami and our ritual of her showing distaste for this person I love in ways that felt routine to us by now. I felt shame for the ways that I had normalized her rejection of this tía. And then I found resentment, tucked into the furthest corner deep inside me. I felt profound resentment for all the forces at play that seek to divide, to conquer us.

I wrote this book to make sense of all those feelings. In these pages I hope to reclaim narratives told to me disguised as well-intentioned warnings about la tía cuir, my tía escandalosa, la loca, and so many other women in my family or chosen family who all deserved better. I am writing this to rip these tías and primas from the clutches of sexism, homophobia, fatphobia, colonization, stigmatization of mental illnesses, male gaze, and rape culture. I am writing this to paint these women as I saw them, as I think about them as an adult, and as I want the world to see them. And maybe I'm romanticizing some of these women I saw peripherally, but fuck it. I am in love with us, and I want a flowery, beautiful book about us that does not pull any punches and jabs hardest at those who have harmed us.

The family is the primary institution for socialization, for acquiring not only language but the various ideological codes of society.

　　　　　　　　　　　　　　　　　—Rosaura Sánchez

I was born in Nicaragua to two very close families, my paternal family of Mojicas and my maternal family of Rodríguezes. It felt like we spent every waking moment together. My maternal grandmother often functioned as a secondary caretaker when my parents had obligations. We saw my paternal grandmother multiple times a week and at her home after church functions. In my papi's family, all of his siblings have given birth to two girls and a boy in their respective family units, and age-wise I was right in the middle of my cousins. I was closest to my cousins on my paternal side, where I had two girl cousins, Dara y Jemima, who were like sisters of mine. Jemima and I were born a day (and a year) apart. On my mami's side of the family, I was one of the oldest cousins in the bunch, but since my mom came from a family filled with women, her side is where I had my most cherished aunts. I was surrounded by women who loved me and helped raise me.

In the US, Latinas in media are stereotyped into three definitive categories: the spicy, hotheaded, curvy, sultry body; the subservient, invisible maid; or the unruly, crime-prone chola/chonga. When they are not portrayed within those narrow perspectives, their Latinidad is stripped from them entirely, and they become part of the status quo. And yet the women I know and love are so much more than those stereotypes. They are so much richer in text and in person than any of those tropes can fully capture, and so in my efforts to keep my memories intact, I am going to incarnate the women who made me—the good, the bad, and the very juicy stuff in between that shaped who I am today.

The last time I visited Nicaragua was in 2016, and I saw a lot of my family. I was older and could really take it all in, but my abuelitas were long gone, and their homes felt different. I also felt different, and maybe it was because I really have changed since the days when we visited more regularly. But I am just like them, in significant ways that felt unseen during that visit. I see so many of the women in my family reflected in my behaviors, core belief systems, and overall views of the world.

The women in my family are vast; they are so vast that they contain multitudes within themselves. The women in my family are far from any stereotypes anyone in Hollywood could ever even fathom. They are funny and wicked and good, but they contain so much pain. I know that because I contain so much pain, and it did not start with me; it is pain passed down.

The women in my family are probably like the women in your family—they are the standard. They are my benchmark, and yet they are products of their trauma, and their resilience to outlive that trauma, and they are kind, but they can be mean. They are beautiful. The women who made me who I am overflow out of the boxes people attempt to put them into.

I have sat in front of my mirror for years trying to decipher where that particular gesture comes from, and why I make that one face when I don't like something. From a pit of information, I am cultivating this book. I have sat in gatherings with tías and primas, my family and my friends' families, my chosen family, and I have watched things I knew to be my normal unfold. And while wonderful and great things happen when families gather, other insidious and less beautiful things often occur too. And this is not about blaming any particular person or persons; this is about expanding the vernacular and truly finding a way to reckon with all that messy shit that makes us who we are. When women's dignity becomes a casualty of a society that normalizes the secondary status of all women, we suffer.

I come from women who protected any sense of dignity they had left with elbow grease and determination. This world prioritizes the men in their lives more than them at every turn. What all this translates to is that the women I love were often very judgmental. Like me, the women in my life created worlds of their own to feel better about where this one had discarded them off to, and they clung to rules. Those rules eroded friendships and were meant to create hierarchies of women among all of us who were disposable. Instead of clinging to one another, we recreated their patterns, and we reinforced their ways of thinking. We found meaning in our oppression and subjugation. And in our own ways, we learned to hate women who stand out; we hate women who dare to defy too loudly; we hate women who dress like they have nothing to lose because we have lost so much; and we hate, hate, and hate ourselves into holes where we raise other haters. We misplace our anger about our roles in society onto one another. We keep ourselves busy hating things about other women when we are upset that our dads discarded us for not being boys, or we feel like having children is our only purpose, or any other limiting gender-based rearing that has stopped us from living. I think if we truly turn to our communities and look at our families, we will find how limited we have been. We are so much more than the santas and the putas. We are limitless. We are the motherfucking Milky Way. We have galaxies within us, and yet we are told we are too loud, too gossipy. That we should sit up straight, do not interrupt, take up space but not too much space, and remember to be perfect. We are all fighting indoctrination, all the time, and the numbing effects of this fight will be brought to the surface in this book.

> *Storytelling is community building.*
>
> —Sharon Lamb

As we continue, I start out by calling us by the names we use for one another—the childless tía, the divorced tía, the matriarch—but really, I am attempting to bring humanity into these labels. I am trying to incarnate theories; I am trying to humanize the pain that is often embodied by our female family lines. Nobody in my book is any one person I have encountered, but an amalgamation of many people to create these specific archetypes. I see so much of myself in so many of these archetypes I have outlined. And yet, as dense and complicated as the tías and primas in this book are, my words are not enough—words fail me. But what I am trying to do is imagine a world where we all get to exist, and I'm speculating on what their existence does to confront our internalized biases as objects of the patriarchy, white supremacy, and capitalism. I'm imagining worlds for us, and

I'm imagining worlds where we are more than objects, we are subjects, and we can exist fully.

This book is a critique of family units that limit our growth while taking into account the fact that these patterns are a direct result of living trauma through national and state abuses, colonization, wars, and institutionalized sexism, racism, and xenophobia. Although this book is centrally about sexism, we have to consider so much more than that. We have not been the creators of systemic oppression, but we for damn sure should be the ones to end the trauma it has inflicted on us.

I want to live in a world where we can see our gente with care and gentleness. I want to peel back layers and ask more questions while elevating our realities as complex and highly nuanced people.

> *You are born to one mother, but if you are lucky, you will have more than one. And among them all you will find most of what you need. Your relationships with todas las madres, the many mothers, will most likely be ongoing ones, for the need for guidance and advisory is never outgrown, nor, from the point of view of women's deep creative life, should it ever be.*
>
> —Clarissa Pinkola Estés

When we left Nicaragua, our migration put the Gulf of Mexico between me and the most important people in my young life. We had the privilege of having papers within a year of having moved, so we could visit. But returning to Nicaragua with a family of five is no cheap ask, so we ended up seeing our relatives there pretty irregularly. And not everyone was able to get visas to visit us, with the exception of my grandparents, since their old age seemed to indicate to the US officials that they had less potential of overstaying their visas. Since then, I have felt that gaping hole left behind after going from being raised by many to being raised by two—a very particular experience.

I would grow to be envious of my immigrant friends who had more family in the US. I once had a boyfriend whose grandparents lived next door to him and his mom. My best friends in Chicago have hordes of cousins, an uncle, and even both grandmothers living a car ride away. It has felt unfair to have family I could not fully interact with because of borders, complicated visa procedures, and expensive airline tickets. It's all bullshit, and borders are inhumane when enforced with an eye toward specific countries while being left practically wide open for others. I have missed my family; I have longed for the women who made the world come alive when we were together.

Every author has biases, and when writing I think it is important that we share our context because it informs our writings. As I stated in the beginning, I am an immigrant and was raised in Latine neighborhoods until I moved away from Miami to Nashville, Tennessee, where I currently live, to attend Vanderbilt University and pursue my master of divinity degree. My family is working-class, and up until college mi papi was a full-time pastor and had a pastor's salary. I was raised by two Spanish-speaking parents who still rely on translators to move through the world, since English does not feel necessary in a place like Miami. My childhood household was very traditional and conservative, based on a patriarchal family structure in which men lead and women follow. This is all evident in how I write about the family dynamics I saw growing up. I commuted to college at a Hispanic-Serving Institution, Florida International University. All of my siblings and I attended the same institution for undergraduate studies, and I am the only member of my family who has a master's degree. I am the oldest daughter but the middle child. Spanish is my first language, but I am a proficient English speaker, and according to some I now have a southern drawl, though I have not noticed it myself. I am a cis woman, and I am bisexual.

I am a non-white, non-Black Latina and identify as brown, even when that is not a recognized racial category. I do not pass as white, and I have never been treated like a white person in Latin America or the US. I never get told I do not look Latina enough, and people are never in disbelief when they hear me identify as Latina. Among my communities, I am the Latina who other bilingual Latines speak to in Spanish first. Among non-Latine white people, I am, phenotypically, the Latina that Fox News uses in its fearmongering reports on immigrants. I am the Latina people think of when they picture someone who is a criminal because that is what they have been told about brownness.

Because we live in a white supremacist society, I have a particular racialized experience. My brownness is not evident when I speak due to any trace of an accent, nor is it evident when I share where I was born; instead, my brownness enters rooms with me. Even when I stand quietly in a corner,

I still get racialized as *other*. I do not look white, I do not pass, so I do not get asked where I am from with genuine curiosity. I have learned how to navigate spaces where I can predict racial biases will bubble up, managing my appearance and learning how to stand up straight like someone who expects respect. And while it doesn't always work, it feels like a shield I work and rework as I learn more and more about internalized biases.

I am Latina enough; that has never been my fight. I have earned that title by shouldering all the negative stereotypes white Latines have readily perpetuated in the media through faking accents and dyeing their hair black or brown to get roles in US shows. They have received the benefits of being "exotic" through a type of brownface, but they do not have to shoulder the negative effects their complicity creates because they are white. It is the Argentinian Anya Taylor-Joy Latina who folks want to meet and prop up as Latine excellence, who reminds them that their whiteness is interesting, at times. It is the Yalitza Aparicio Latina whose success is perceived as an anomaly and whose Indigeneity is mocked. I have a particular set of experiences from growing up looking like my Indigenous ancestors in a cultura that wants to forget who our countries belonged to before our colonizers came. White Latines show disdain toward me as much as non-Latine white people do. I am a past they never want to remember, and that is what I mean when I say that I am brown—not a metaphor but a living, breathing experience of otherness.

This positionality 100 percent impacts how I write and why I write what I do. I worked closely with the illustrator Josie

Del Castillo to make the accompanying illustrations for each chapter as wide-ranging as possible in body diversity, race, and racially diverse facial features and storylines. Yet there are limitations to my lived experiences as a non-white and non-Black Latina, and naming that feels pertinent. I do not write about Latinidad as the be-all and end-all; rather, I am but a comma in a long list of Latines writing about our experiences through different lenses.

Spanglish comes out of me from time to time, and I do not italicize my Spanish words. To me, as a fully bilingual person, I do not denote the foreign language usage because neither is foreign to me, and my reader will understand that. I switch what words I use in Spanish; it is more organic than anything else. When a particular story feels tender and close, I use my traditional papi and mami, but if the topic feels more matter-of-fact, I use other monikers. This applies to tía, aunt, abuelita, grandmother, prima, and cousin. This often happens without me thinking, and going back and changing how the stories came out of me feels disingenuous.

> *Conversation and social interaction are a major part of women's lives and gesture and voice are crucial to these communications.*
> —Devra Anne Weber

My writings are meant to be said out loud and discussed. I am inspired by oral storytelling traditions that I grew up with at home and Pentecostal church sermons that have a similar rhythm to them. I enjoy a good cadence. I enjoy rich allegories. When publishing opened its doors to me, I made a promise to myself to run through those doors with ferocious abandon, carrying my heritage and everyone who made me on my back. If democratizing knowledge is the long-term goal, then repackaging these theories in story form feels important for connecting to people who grew up with stories like I did. I write books to translate academic theory for folks who don't, can't, or won't read academic books but love a good story.

I write for the masses because somebody's got to dig through the muddy waters of academese and find the gems that feel resonant. My intention lies in the fact that when I finally learned all this academic theory, which ultimately made my brain create new neural pathways to imagine new realities and make sense of my own experiences, I had to sacrifice a lot of myself along the way. I lost myself trying to gain access to inaccessible spaces. It is unjust to foist that expectation of self-abnegation on Black, Indigenous, and people of color from working-class backgrounds.

I write the books I needed and should have gotten to read, and not by navigating impossible obstacles to reach ivory towers, but at my local public library. I write the books I wish I would've stumbled upon. I write the books I needed to wake up. I write books honoring how my people communicate lessons, warnings, and histories.

Ultimately, in writing this book I hope that the Gulf of Mexico won't feel so large to traverse. I hope that wherever your family or chosen family is—whether right in the same city as you, through your phone if they live in another country, or in your altars at home where you honor their contributions to your life—you may deepen your connection to them that transcends obligation. May this book lead you back to them with new words, new ways of reflecting on memories, and new tools for how we can do better.

1

LA MATRIARCH

Since I am a woman, people—men and women
alike—drink from me. I am the eternal well of pathos.
(It Is You, My Sisterm, Who Must Be Protected)
—Cherríe Moraga

LET ME TELL YOU ABOUT MY MATRIARCH, THE MATRIARCH AS I KNEW her. She passed away too soon at fifty-five. I remember the suddenness of it all. The summer she died I was turning fifteen. Since I was so young when she passed, I think I have grown accustomed to romanticizing her. I have not held her in all her glory with my now thirty-eight-year-old eyes, hands, and olfactory sense. I have her scripted in my memories—her scent as I knew it as a girl and teenager, her hands, how she looked, and what she wore.

My memories and reflections of things I saw at that young age have created this bubble where she resides. That is the point of this book: to conjure her and women like her. To keep the memories of our matriarchs alive for future generations who will not get to meet them, but who should have access to the folk tales they would have inspired if our stories were the ones centered and widely told.

My matriarch was mighty. She was the measure we are to live by for the women in my family. She exemplified the aspiration that everyone tries to live up to. She balanced a lot of realities gracefully, or at least we saw her as doing it all better than anyone. She was our dignity personified. And all we could do was try to live up to those impossible standards, or perish trying.

Mi matriarca was named Rosa Esperanza, and she was sturdy. She had a thick, curly head of hair that she permed back in the 1950s and never stopped maintaining since. She stood a solid five foot three when she wore her two-inch heels, which was always. Her heels told you a lot about her, as both she and her shoes were sensible, durable, and dependable. She wore a skirt every day. Her nails were often done, she slept with curlers, and she woke up at 5 o'clock every single morning to sweep and mop her home. When everyone finally started waking up, she was already bathed and dressed, and the coffee was ready. Her home was immaculate yet warm and inviting.

If you were invited into her home, you would know all this to be true. As soon as you walked through the doorway, you felt like you were exactly where you needed to be. It was a narrow house where each room led to the next. You walked in and were met with four mecedoras where she would sit at night to chat. Most evenings, she would drag those mecedoras to the front porch and rock. This time of sitting was cherished. A matriarch is never resting for too long. When you see her kick up her feet, you notice it; it is rare. When she finally sits among us, she feels like us and less like the deity she moves as on a regular basis. You have to be endless to do what she does. She does too much. The standard is impossible.

In my abuelita Rosa's home, once you passed the mecedoras you were met with the TV room, and past that was the kitchen. Beyond the kitchen was her dining room. I can close my eyes and see it clearly: doilies everywhere, framed pictures of all her kids and grandkids. Her home was not grand, but it was the safest place on earth. It was safe because she felt like a trustworthy protector. A matriarca and her home are one, and everyone knows it.

She would scurry. She was always scurrying. She was a proud hostess. When she made nacatamales, she made all of them special. She did not write our names on banana leaves, but she might as well have. When they came out, and we all waited around the table for our serving, she would peel back the banana leaf and immediately know which nacatamal was made for whom. "La niña solamente quiere maza y papas," "A Richard le das más chancho," "A la Blanquita le gustan las chiltomas," "Al abuelo le das la que tiene muchas papas." She knew our orders better than we did, and she always aimed to please without ever spoiling us. She was perfection. She was a magician. She worked hard to become this to all of us—indispensable.

My matriarch was so abundant that she became the neighborhood matriarch. She knew if someone had lost a loved one, and she would make time to visit and bring them meals. And if she did not have time to do that, she would send one of her kids or grandkids with prepped meals, condolences, and a promise to visit soon. My matriarch knew when a family was in need, and even given the little she had, she always managed to carve out some for them. Nothing ever fell through the cracks. Mi matriarca was a saint. The way the neighbors spoke of her character was something to make you puff your chest out. You'd proudly say, "Esa es mi abuelita" con gusto.

My matriarca was a business owner. An origin story I heard often from my tías about my abuelita was that back when she was first married, my abuelo's wandering eye made her flee her hometown. Her mother, my great-grandmother, told her that if she stayed in their small town, she was going to lose her husband. And so, my abuelita Rosa packed up her children and husband and moved the entire family to the big city, the capital of my country called Managua. And when my grandfather weaponized his salary against her, counting every penny he gave her and their children, she decided to make her own money. That was the prudent thing to do; that is what women like her do. A matriarca is like that. She will not be beaten, and she will not lose.

From nothing, mi matriarca started a pulpería from her own home. I remember seeing her store grow. It was already a business by the time I was born, but it grew bigger every year. At first she sold baked goods, fresh tortillas, nacatamales, and Coca-Cola products. And by the time she passed away, she had added a room to the front of the house that was the official storefront. She even had display carts she rolled out in the mornings filled with nail polishes and school supplies. People in her neighborhood, where owning a car is still a rarity, subsisted off her store. They could get whatever they needed from her, and if she did not have it upon request, she would make sure to have it next time. She sold everything from picos to cigarettes and lottery tickets, crema and queso, and fresh hot tortillas. Her business grew and grew.

My matriarca never left her husband. With as many children as they had, it was "practical" to stay. I remember telling my parents, at age six, that I did not like visiting my abuelita's home. When they asked me why, I said it was because she and my grandpa were always fighting. I did not like it. But today I understand, and I have a lot more grace for what she went through. She stayed, but she was no pendeja. She earned her way into her career path, she made herself a force to be reckoned with, and she fought. Her fighting spirit scared me because it felt like a warning I could not wrap my head around.

Matriarchs do not reach their status without a deep understanding of compromise. I think mi matriarca knew when to bend, and when to push. She knew the systems in place and how to survive them.

> *She knows her husband too well to let herself still be intimidated by him, she avoids his embraces, she carves out—in friendship, indifference, or hostility—a real life of her own alongside him; if he declines more quickly than she, she takes the lead in the couple.*
>
> —Simone de Beauvoir

People often talk about being their ancestor's wildest dreams, and I think about whether mi matriarca would even approve of my decisions today. Because I do not compromise; I do not even think I fully understand the concept anymore. I see rules, and I poke holes in them. I left a seemingly loving marriage because I wanted more. I have abandoned the idea of having my own children because I want to nurture the child within me who did not get nurtured. I have not lived traditionally for the sake of advancing respectfully. And because of all those things, I have come to understand that mi matriarca would turn in her grave if she knew the extent of my fighting spirit. When I stepped back and saw what a matriarca means, what it really means to be on top, I realized how infinitely hard it must have been for her. The shoulders I stand on are mighty, but I think it cost her everything. Heavy lies the crown.

The family matriarch is an interesting archetype within our communities because there are elements of traditional/dominant gender roles that matriarchs enforce and that grant them this status of matriarch. It is often a silent matriarchy that everyone knows is real, but is seldom openly discussed so as not to offend the matriarch's husband, if he is still around. A husband who is often lying to himself about his role in their relationship and family unit, even when it is abundantly clear.

A great majority of individuals enforce an unspoken rule in the culture as a whole that demands we keep the secrets of patriarchy, thereby protecting the rule of the father.

This rule of silence is upheld when the culture refuses
everyone easy access even to the word "patriarchy."

—bell hooks

Her role as matriarch is seldom openly acknowledged because of traditional/dominant gender roles, and they endorse this balancing act. The silent emotional labor that carries her family is not even fully understood until she inevitably passes. Her passing leaves a void. The void is indicative of her matriarchal role. The matriarca shows a strength that other women in the family try to emulate. There is this invaluable element to who she is to all of us, both individually and as a whole.

We know it when it comes to gathering for holidays, and we know it when it comes to conflict within the family too. The matriarch is the official gatherer and hostess of the family, and the matriarch is also oftentimes the one who will step into conflicts to seek a resolution or validate one side over another, thereby ending said conflict. She is the sounding board and the balanced perspective.

The matriarch is the one who passes down family recipes and skills, and she even somehow manages to always have her own money stashed away for a rainy day because she understands that her importance is financial, emotional, psychological, and physical. All this is what makes this tía, because she is someone's tía, multifaceted and extremely important. The matriarch is oftentimes older, and very often a grandmother figure, but like I said earlier, all women within our communities are someone's tía. My abuelita Rosa was the matriarch, though I would not say the same about my other abuelita, Cándida. Not all grandmothers are matriarchs, and not all families have clear matriarchs. Some women will never become matriarchs. I will never become a matriarch.

Mi abuelita Rosa was decidedly a matriarch because of how she moved in and out of tradition with the confidence of someone who needs no one but knows everyone needs her. Mi abuelita Rosa owned her own pulpería and had her own bank account. Having her own money like she did, during the times she lived in, was the biggest act of resistance I saw growing up.

As much as a matriarch appears "traditional," her devotion to a man is conditional. A matriarch has learned the hard way that she cannot rely on her husband. Her devotion is out of a sense of duty, not actually tangible on a daily basis. I did not understand true love between a man and a woman because all around me I had seen women stay with men they did not seem to love. What I understood about women my grandmother's age was sadness and hard work.

> *Heartbroken women in longtime marriages or partnerships rarely leave their men. They learn to make an identity out of their suffering, their complaint, their bitterness.*
>
> —bell hooks

A matriarch can be a matriarch of a family even when she is in another country. Our matriarch was involved in our lives even when we moved to the United States. My matriarch sewed all my uniforms until middle school from swatches my mami sent to her. She visited a lot and was always in the know about our lives even when we avoided the mandatory telephone calls with Grandma. My matriarch sent us money and called us on all our birthdays, including mi papi's. When she passed and those phone calls stopped coming in, we all felt it. That is the power of a matriarch.

A matriarch is irreplaceable; that is a key component of a matriarch. Once she is gone, rarely can someone else step up and fill the hole left behind. What ends up happening is that families become aware of the void, and they try to fill it within their own family units. When my matriarch died, my own mami became acutely aware of her new role as the matriarch of our home. She became a matriarch in the making. She spoke about the newfound responsibility she felt.

I have seen mi mami's resolve since her own mother is no longer alive, and she has had to step up, for us. She harnessed all my abuelita's strengths, and she became who she relied on her entire life. She became the pillar in our lives, a pillar she modeled after her own. The way she insists on never becoming the enemy of the spouses of her children is a strategy of hers. A matriarca is a peacemaker. And although she can pack some heat, she will lead with care for those she has chosen to care for.

Matriarchs tend to be very stubborn, and they often evolve into kinder people as their grandchildren come into the world. That is a key trait of a matriarch. Matriarchs also have no real favorites, and their love is so vast that they even care for others outside their own families. My matriarch was not only mine; she was also the community's matriarch. When she died, the entire neighborhood mourned her death because she had more than one family—she was responsible for many.

When mi matriarca died, nobody was expecting it. She did such an incredible job of being strong and helpful to everyone that she developed this *fun* little habit of doing little to nothing for herself and seldom asking for help. That is why I call her a saint: she suffered so that others would not. She had been diagnosed with hypertension, and ultimately she died of organ failure and complications related to a bunch of little things that all went wrong at the same time. She did not have to die, but she did. All she did her entire life was try to live up to these impossible standards, and she perished trying. Being our impossible standard cost her her life.

We were in Miami when we got a phone call that she had been taken to the hospital. I remember my parents driving to Miami International Airport and begging someone at a ticket counter to help mi mami get to Nicaragua. The same-day rates for buying a plane ticket anywhere are astronomical, especially for international flights, but my parents thought they could plead their emergency to the airline directly. They tried to get on a standby flight. They tried to connect to their compassion. They failed at first, but through a lot of mutual aid and community support, they gathered the money. My grandmother died the night before my mother flew out to be by her side. It was a matter of days from her being hospitalized to eventually passing.

Nobody knew how sick she had been. Nobody knew that she was in pain for as long as she was. Nobody knew to be prepared. It took the air out of all our lives. One day, you have this strong tree with deep roots holding on to every member of your family, and the next day the tree is gone. It felt like we were all floating. And no one knew how to comfort one another; we did not know how to grieve together. I remember mi mami sobbing for an entire year. She would just cry while making dinner; she would cry while watching television; she would stay in bed and cry all day.

A matriarca is missed because a matriarch is exceptional. She is the reason for so many of your happy memories, and you don't even realize it until she is gone. I will never forget that birthday because mi abuelita died on my quince. Most Latinas from Catholic families get a quinceañera, but I got a new ancestor at mi quince. We felt her loss for a while. I still feel that loss.

When a matriarch leaves the living world, she leaves a crater behind.

To the matriarch, I say: the best lesson you can carry with you is that taking care of yourself should be part of the community service that you so willingly do for others. Your absence will always be felt in the communities you helped and loved, so love us back by loving yourself in the best ways you know how. Imagine the most important person in your life passing, and then multiply that tenfold—that is what it feels like to lose a matriarch. At every graduation, wedding, birth, and even funeral we all beckon you. We all say your name to speak you into existence. We say, "Sería bien tuani si la abuelita/mi mami/la Rosita estuviera aquí..."

If you ever find yourself in a matriarchal role, know that while we all depend on you, we also need you to live a long life. Being so essential means offering a great deal to a whole lot of people. When that much of you is poured out to others, it is self-sacrifice. That overabundance of love has to flow back to yourself. Take care of yourself. We deserve to have you with us for as long as humanly possible, but we cannot have you with us if you are not taking care of your own needs. And you need to ask for more. Learn to say, "Necesito ayuda." You are the standard, and teaching us how to live long lives is good for everyone involved. We cannot live up to your impossible standard.

> *Domestic work is not viewed as a job when performed by a wife or female partner but often as a labor of love.*
> —Justin Charlebois

To those who love a matriarch, if the words you use to talk about your matriarch are similar to my words—"saint," "irreplaceable," "the standard"—then rein in your overdependence. A matriarch's biggest flaw can be that she cannot say "no" when she is needed, and your biggest strength must become doing things yourself, so she does not have to, and insisting that she take care of herself. A matriarch needs help, and she may not have the words to ask for it because life told her that if she wanted something done well, she had to do it herself. So teach her that she has help now. Help her learn to rely on you. Become reliable.

I lost out on growing up with my matriarch nearby, but I cherish my memories I have of our time together. And while she might disapprove of me if she were alive, I live to honor her. I honor her by saying "no" a lot more than I was socialized to do, and I proclaim her name into spaces that require more of me than I know I can give. Learning from her mistakes is the best gift I can give to an ancestor I lost too early to the toll of expected female labor.

2

THE YOUNG TÍA

One is not born, but rather becomes, a woman.

—Simone de Beauvoir

L ET ME TELL YOU ABOUT MY YOUNG TÍA, OR AS I LIKE TO CALL HER, MY cool tía. Her name is Carolina. When I was little, and before I could fully pronounce her name, I called her my tía Calina. She is eight years younger than my mom, so in my oldest memories of her, she was still living at home with my grandparents, going to school, working, and dating.

I refer to her as the cool tía because that is who she was, and in so many ways, that is who she continues to be when I think of the cool tía, even as she has evolved.

The cool tía understands your parents and speaks to them like she is a worthy match as they banter and joke together. The familiarity of having known them before they were your parents lends itself to this kind of ease. She watched them date as teenagers, and that breaks a lot of walls down. The level of knowing is evident in the ways their bodies relax around one another; the intimacy that is shared among these lifelong friends is unmatched.

Yet, she does not always feel like an adult. She feels like an in-between figure. My tía Calina was not one of them; she felt more like one of us kids. But she also was not entirely one of us. Her childhood, her girlhood, felt fresh. It was like adulting was cosplay to her, but really she was more like us than them.

I remember this one story about her, a story I heard told and retold almost every time I saw my parents and tía get together. When my family gathers, we pass down stories and construct ourselves for the young ones watching, the ones who weren't witnesses to these stories as they were lived. The story goes that my mom and dad had broken up because my mom heard a rumor that my dad was seen with another girl. They attended different private Catholic schools, and word got around about anything that occurred in either one. My mom went to an all-girls school, and word usually got to her extra fast, especially when it came to her boyfriend. With the news of my father's "betrayal," my mom broke up with my dad. As my dad retells it, he did nothing, and mi mami was just very jealous. He was simply standing next to a girl, and according to him, her spies had exaggerated the events. Innocent until proven guilty is his stance. As my mother retells this part, she claims that all the rumors were true and my dad had been caught. My mom always drops the name of her reliable source, and my dad is always quick to discredit this source with his own tales of her unreliability. After a few eye rolls and laughs, they both agree on what happened next: it was my young tía who resuscitated their relationship after this incident.

After they broke up, my tía Calina wrote my dad a letter. Well, it was more like she had painted a painting since I believe she was seven years old. She is a kid, in this story. In this painting, she drew herself crying as my dad was driving away in his blue pickup truck. On this painting, she wrote a note begging my dad to fix things with my mom and come back to visit her.

In that story, she is the hero. She is touted as the reason my parents are still together. She is important in that story. She is also about the same age I was when I first remember hearing that story. That is what this tía does; she makes the children feel consequential in a life that oftentimes makes us feel inconsequential. Her presence is profound. This is what I mean when I say that she feels like one of us. This tía has always felt like one of us.

We feel comradery with this tía. She plays with the kids. She indulges them, due to her proximity, but also because she recently was a kid herself. Her memories are still vivid of having felt the "unfair" treatment of parents. It is probably because her adolescence feels a hopscotch jump away, if not still present. She can still remember her curfews; she may still have a curfew. She can still remember the rules set by adults and resents them, or she may even still live by the rules of her parents.

She hesitates to become a woman; she frets at still being only a child; she has already left her past; she is not yet committed to a new life.

—Simone de Beauvoir

Ella te entiende, y te quiere for that reason.

My young tía was more of a confidant than any other adult in my life. I viewed this tía as more like a friend, my first adult friend. I also understood that she loved me, very dearly, like mi mami did. I understood she felt responsible for me, watchful. And she seemed especially invested in me and my happiness. It felt intimate because it felt intertwined. She saw me and then saw the me I could become. Young tías do this. They set their sights on you and lock you in. You are theirs because you are their sibling's child. One and the same. And this may not be something that every young tía will feel, but the one I am writing about feels this way. She is special.

My young tía was a revolutionary, an activist. She dropped out of college to serve as a sort-of reading tutor in rural parts of our country, Nicaragua. After the Sandinistas won the revolution, they set out to teach Nicaraguans how to read through a campaign called the Nicaraguan Literacy Campaign. In 1979, it is believed that a larger percentage of our population was illiterate. Because we had lived in a dictatorship, and dictators do not care about the lives of their subjects, this illiteracy was of no consequence. It made mules out of people, and that was something our dictators praised.

And so, our newly minted revolutionary president set out to change that. The literate population was encouraged to sign up to educate our gente. My young tía was one of those people who saw the importance of reading and giving that access to people, and she was great with kids. What that meant was that while there were many adults who were also being taught to read, she focused on teaching children.

As she did this work, it developed into her job; she became something like a social worker. These programs developed into more steady lines of work. She spent years checking in on her students and giving them more books to read. I have this photograph of her ingrained in my mind because I have stared at it so many times. In this picture, she is wearing her Sandinista gear, surrounded by mountains in la jungle, with the biggest smile on her face. There is no one around; it's just her—badass and bonita. She looks so young to me now, but also so free.

She made me believe that being an adult was fun and that it could be an adventure. She made adulthood appear like something to aspire to, not dread. Her life felt full of playfulness. This particular tía does things like that; she has a life full of things aside from kids and bills. This particular tía feels fascinating because even when she begins to step into the drudgery of responsibilities, the memories of her still make her less like a full-fledged adult, less like your parents. There is something precious about what she illustrates to the young children in her life, something to emulate and something to protect about adulthood. Capitalism tries to steal our multitudes and our expansiveness from us; we become robots of labor when in reality we are so much more, and the young tía gives us glimpses into that possibility.

Her clothes are sexier. She wears bold colors and seems to stand out, wants to stand out. She also might wear more makeup and indulges in things your mami is too busy to indulge in. Your young tía's liberties are seductive, making you want to be just like her. I remember when she said her favorite color was purple. I made that my favorite color for all of elementary school. When other girls loved pink, I loved purple just as much as I loved my young tía. In actuality, the color purple did nothing for me, but it incarnated her for me when borders felt like knives and her distance from me felt unbearable. While I did not have her near me, I could always wear purple and keep her nearby.

Compared to my churchgoing, pastoral parents, she was living her life unleashed. I did not yet understand that I was my parents' metaphorical leash, one of their many leashes. It is not that this tía will always be unburdened; eventually, this tía grows up. This tía dates right before your very eyes, but it is exciting! You get to witness something that your parents only talk about, and if you are lucky, you might even get to be a chaperone of sorts. In some ways, she inducted me into the traditional heterosexual path for women by inviting me to observe her transitions.

> *The destiny that society traditionally offers women is marriage.*
>
> —Simone de Beauvoir

Because of my age and hers, I was often the ideal chaperone when her boyfriend would come to take my young tía out on a date. Because no one had a car on my mami's side of the family in Nicaragua, and my young tía's boyfriend also did not own a car, they walked to their dates. They had met while doing their revolutionary work. He was an activist too. On their dates, they would often walk to an ice cream parlor

near my abuelita's house in a neighborhood in Managua called
Bello Horizonte. Since they were both activists and social
workers, their cheap dates were ideal.

I like to think I hazed him to ensure his commitment,
as my little sister would do years later when I was around my
young tía's age and I dated a boy. I would walk alongside them,
and within two blocks of my abuelita's home, where we had
just departed, I would fake exhaustion to avoid walking the
rest of the way. This would always result in me getting picked
up and carried by my young tía's boyfriend the entire way to
and from the local ice cream parlor, pastry shop, or just the
corner quesillos stand.

I remember that he smelled like cologne and sweat, and
they seemed to be happy. Their youth was enviable, by both
the children who were still under the watch of our parents and
by the adults who were probably enjoying not having to watch
us themselves whenever we were with her. But to me, she was
living a dream, a goal I was taught to mirror. And I got to participate. He was our boyfriend, our friend who happened to be
a boy. They dated how I would eventually be told to date.

The fate of your young tía feels written in stone. She will
wed. She will have her own children. She will become an adult
with real adult responsibilities, and she will change. And yet
you will always remember her as she was when you were most
impressionable.

I remember mi tía's music. You will remember your young
tía's music. My young tía had a Gloria Trevi phase. She would
turn on the television and go through a few channels trying
to find a channel that was playing music videos, and then we

would wait for what felt like an eternity for the song "Pelo Suelto" to come on. Thankfully, around that time it was always on somewhere, so we didn't have to wait as long as it often felt. And as soon as "Pelo Suelto" came on, we would stomp our feet on the tile in mi abuelita's home and sing right along with Gloria. I knew all the lyrics. We would scream, "Voy a traer el pelo suelto / voy a ser siempre como quiero / aunque me tachen de indecente!" It was like we were both screaming for our emancipation, but from very different perspectives. At that age I could not imagine what she would have needed to be emancipated from, but today I understand a little more. My young tía grew up right before my very eyes, and often my young brain could barely keep up.

Young tías are magic. They can bring so much joy to the little humans in their lives. Young tías can see humanity and reasoning through the eyes of children. As a child it is easy to feel inconsequential, sometimes from having adults treat you like you have nothing important to say due to lack of experience and overall ageism. My young tía would ask me questions and look me in the eyes when we spoke like every single thing I said was important. I wanted to ensure that when I spoke it was with intention because I knew she was actually listening. She made me think, and she introduced me to a new way of being. Young tías give their nieces, nephews, and niblings that gift, the gift of making them feel witnessed. In my patriarchal household, she defended me when my older brother got too nasty with me. When my parents overlooked behavior, she stepped up. She took my side and would often scold my brother for being what she would call a "jayán," with a face that backed her words. She was a protector, a confidant, and also an adult who saw me as someone who was her own person, and not as someone who was not yet a full person. She did not push me to grow up, nor did she push me to stay small—she accompanied me. Young tías can have that effect.

I had a young tía, one who was adventurous and good. A young tía who reminded me that mi mami was a sister and not just mi mami. I had a young tía who taught me that having fun is not just something children do because she showed me that adults can have fun and laugh till they cry, and they can wear purple shoes and dance to music until they are out of breath. This tía teaches you a lot—that is part of the experience with her.

I had a young tía who taught me how to be a young tía myself. When I see my nieces and nephews and niblings, I hope to provide for them what my own tía provided for me: healthy, fun exchanges with a young adult. I would go through most of my childhood having adults react in punitive ways toward me, till I grew old enough to defend myself. I would go through most of my childhood interacting with adults with a lot of their trauma that they, intentionally or not, dumped on me. I would go through most of my childhood being dismissed by adults. I remember mi tía as a person who acknowledged my humanity even if I was just a kid. When I think about gentle parenting, my only example is my young tía. She serves as a model.

To the family of the young tía, through her youth we can mine so much about how children want to be treated, and how they should be treated. Allow her existence in your life to inform how we treat the little ones in our lives. They are consequential and should feel that way, and if they do not, we need to make that more explicit. Your young tía may be a model for your relationships with the children of your siblings and those of your close friends. Take all that energy. Harness it.

I would grow up to want to emulate my own tía jovencita; I would grow up cherishing the parts of her that life had not taken from her yet. I hope the family of the young tía realizes how much possibility her existence has for your children. Encourage their bond. Serve as a silent spectator for what will unfold before your very eyes.

To the young tía, eventually you will grow up. My young tía is now a full adult, married to a man with her own adult children, and she denies she ever wore purple heels and danced to Gloria Trevi. Society rewards a particular kind of womanhood, and she has grown old enough to experience that personally. Society has taught her what it will eventually teach us all, though some of us try to shield ourselves from its grasp. Today, my young tía feels like a figment of my imagination, until some other prima will remind me that she, too, had similar memories of our young tía. Us primas who are around the same age, we remember who she was to us and why it was important for us, even if she disavows it all.

To the young tía, your nieces and nephews and niblings will notice the ways that you step into adulthood; allow their questions about your internal shifts to inform those shifts. Maybe they have something of value to reflect about our larger society. I implore you to dare to remember who you were and what that meant. I gently ask that you push against these norms, for your sake and theirs.

To the young tía, you are invaluable to your young, impressionable family members who admire you. Remember that wherever you go and in whatever you do. You will never be forgotten. In fact, you may be remembered as the most significant adult relationship in the lives of your nieces, nephews, and niblings. Give yourself a pat on the back for being the most extraordinary adult many of us have ever met, and maybe will ever meet again. You have become a standard, and that is no easy feat.

3

LA PRIMA PERFECTA

The word "good," when used to describe girls, has little to do with real morality and lots to do with social norms. I think of social norms as rules about what's "proper" or acceptable, rather than rules about what's morally right. These rules rein in women and girls and restrict their development in important ways.

—Sharon Lamb

BEFORE I JUMP INTO THIS, I THINK IT IS IMPORTANT TO NOTE THAT NOT all of your family are your friends. More often than not, family does not mean friends. And sometimes, friends can become chosen family. But even more so, some relatives who are around your same age can become your friends. I have two cousins I genuinely think I would befriend outside of the family dynamics. One of them is mi prima perfecta.

In fact, we are the closest of all the cousins. When we were little, we were only ever allowed to have sleepovers at each other's homes back when I lived in Nicaragua. Our moms had so much confidence in the way they raised us individually that they allowed us to be close since they trusted that the other was going to do well by their daughter. We both have strict mamis, and strict parents in general, but specifically strict moms. I often think that if mi papi had raised my siblings and me, we would have had a different childhood. A significantly less strict childhood. The strictness of our upbringings was mother-led. We were also the oldest daughters, so how we acted seemed to be very much a primary preoccupation of our parents, who felt pressures around how they were reflected in their roles. Our behavior was closely tracked; if they could have monitored our thoughts, they would have done that too.

If you ever see this prima, she is usually seated somewhere. She does not want to be the center of attention; it is like she wants to not be seen. But she is always visible; adults know where she is because she is the example they want their daughters to emulate. A heavy burden is the one she carries.

I can clearly picture her in any given room. Her arms are crossed, and she is keeping to herself. The prima perfecta aims to please and be respectful. When she is speaking to an adult, she uses the correct usted. She looks down often to show respect or submission. She uses titles, regardless of the setting. If someone is a doctor, they are a doctor everywhere they go. If someone is a pastor, they are a pastor even if you see them in the grocery store. If someone is married, they are a doña or señora by marriage or age, and that is their proper and earned honorific.

Being good is a driving force.

This prima dresses modestly. Her hems are right above the knee, and not an inch higher. Her pants are never too tight. She does not wear tight clothes at all. Remember, she is reflecting "proper" parenting. The colors she works within are muted, nothing flashy. Her hair is always done, never unkempt. She knows what that means, and she works within the rules set up by society but also upheld by her parents.

In many cultures, there is an expectation when a female child is born that she is or will become a certain type of person, acting in a certain time-honored way, that she will have a certain set of values, which if not identical to the family's, then at least based on the family's values, and which at any rate will not rock the boat. These expectations are defined very narrowly when one or both parents suffer from a desire for "the angel child," that is, the "perfect" conforming child.

—Clarissa Pinkola Estés

You can always count on the perfect prima to offer a helping hand and emotional labor, and to be available at a moment's notice if you phone her to tell her you need help. She is solid.

And she has her own interests, perfectly normal interests. My prima la perfecta loves jewelry—dainty, delicate, and just the proper amount of femininity. She wears studs and chains with a small pendant. On the side, she makes jewelry and sells it to earn some extra money to help her family. She seldom wears makeup, and when she does, it is light makeup, a little blush and some gloss. She is enhancing her natural beauty, never creating an illusion of being anything she is not.

When she has a crush on someone, she whispers about it. She does not make it obvious, and she does not pursue; that is just not who she is. She expects respectful courting, and nothing else will do. She does not date; she is expected to marry the first suitable man who presents himself. She is taught to expect that, and she has learned to do as she is told. She will not be caught in a compromising situation. She respects her parents too much to allow anyone to devalue her. That is the framing she operates within; she must. That is the only way all this works, if she believes all these myopic frameworks that are meant to control her and keep her good. And the minute she shows any resistance, the consequences are felt all around her. She knows better than to disobey and question what she has been told.

She is quick to get a job; she signals reliability to employers. And she is good at her job, as predicted. She does what she is told without hesitation. The prima who is perfect is the pride of her parents. They pat themselves on their backs because they raised someone who honors them how they want. They get compliments from other adults, throughout her entire life, that they did well. They love how she makes them look. They are model parents, according to everyone who sees la perfecta.

Good children were the adored and treasured possessions of good, loving adults.

—Elisabeth Young-Bruehl

La perfecta never complains; la perfecta never says no; la perfecta will wring herself of all she has in order to please; la perfecta is the shining standard to those raising little girls. In some significant ways, the ones who are able to hold on to all that perfectionism throughout their entire lives, they become the perfect matriarchs. A matriarch is perfect much like la prima perfecta is groomed to be. A matriarch is a mother. A woman who is perfect is nine times out of ten going to become a mother—this type of gendered perfection is only perfection if she follows social rules around what is right and what is the correct order of things for her gender. Marriage first, then children—there is a proper order to things, and she knows to do everything in her power to maintain such order.

La perfecta is strong. The necessity for strength is both for herself and her ability to navigate her family. She is a shoulder to cry on. She will give sound advice. She is constantly working and giving and performing up to the high standards set only for daughters. She has to be good; she has to be inviolable; she has to be dependable.

We all understand that, but not all of us can be that perfect; we say this to satisfy ourselves. I could not stay the perfect daughter. I buckled and slammed my entire body straight into a train of socializing when I asked for a divorce. I could not balance it all because it was a balance of things set for me and not by me. And once I realized how little of my life was actually mine, I set out to burn it all to the ground, and I got singed but I got out. I have heard it said that it was all because I was not hit enough by my parents, corrected enough, or tamed by a strong enough man—the blame can be placed anywhere when perfection is required of girls more than boys.

Boys, in my context, are perfect from the minute they are born. They are perfect when they try, and they are perfect when they fail. They are perfect by becoming the ones their mothers place their unmet expectations of men upon. They are perfect because they belong to their mothers. They are only shunned when they hate their mothers, but every other fault can be forgiven and explained away. My brother has always been perfect in my mother's eyes. I have understood that since I was a little girl. I had to earn perfection, and even then it was a tenuous position.

> *Research shows that at an early age, girls more than boys learn to mask anger in their facial expressions. In experiments where researchers disappoint children, preschool girls contain themselves more in the presence of an adult.*
>
> —Sharon Lamb

At family gatherings, the perfect prima is eventually so reliably good that she blends into the furniture. The other women seldom bother with her because she is not going to do anything bad; she does not need advice because nothing new is happening to her. We all know what she is up to, and we think we know who she is. We assume she is okay because she tells us so with a smile on her face.

La perfecta is often going to be the oldest daughter. I don't make the rules; I just watch it all unfold time and time again. The thing about being the oldest prima is that when she came into this world, our world, she was given all the advice and molded to fit everyone's expectations, and she was tough and somehow figured it out. She explains everyone to everyone, meaning she has figured us all out. She has had to learn how to read people, and it has become instinctual. She reads situations and figures out where she is needed the most and when she can disappear.

There is a lot at play with the perfect prima. She received the same messaging we all got, but she received it the most by birth order, and she ran with it. Her doting behavior should not be confused with goodness, as we are so prone to do. Rather, we should be asking more questions about her childhood and her parents. The model parents we think we are to replicate, whether intentionally or not, may have made her believe that being good meant she was worthy of love, and there is something so insidious about that correlation.

Perfectionism is not something to admire; perfectionism reflects pressures to perform for others, and that is not a sign of a healthy adult person. More so, it is indicative of traumatic parenting. La prima perfecta may not even be aware that she has internal needs after a lifetime of burying them. And I definitively believe it is the parents who are to blame. Yes, the parents who are praised for having raised such an example of a daughter—those very parents are to blame.

I have grown hesitant to praise parents for what I perceive to be good kids, kids who do not distract, kids who blend in with the furniture, or kids who do not break things. Because while some kids may be naturally quieter, most children learn through mistakes, and they are loud and they are messy and they are not perfect and quiet. It is natural in childhood development to make mistakes, and quiet kids who never make mistakes tell me they are scared.

It has taken years for me to override my own lens for what a "good kid" is. I can still recount the attributes because I have always understood that those were the behaviors I was to embody. I was to be smart but not too smart; funny but in the right moments; seen but not heard, especially around other adults; able to play alone wherever mi mami took me. I was supposed to do what I was told, the first time I was told to do it. I was supposed to never interrupt adults when they were speaking. I was supposed to display happiness, above all else. I was supposed to be good, never forgetting to say por favor y gracias, con permiso, and if you went above and beyond, it was better—muchísimas gracias. If I forgot, even just once, it merited an excruciating ear-pulling or hitting. The threat of violence for not being good is incentive enough, you'd think, to kill off any curiosity and silence any budding intelligence.

But it does not always work; some of us become experts at our secrets. I learned to hide parts of myself. I learned what parts were not reflective of a good kid, and then learned to perform for adults. I think that is why la prima perfecta and I were so close growing up: I knew all the best spots to hide and never get caught. We relied on our assumed goodness and stuck together for double the protection. The good girls were never going to do something bad, right? I was always quick to find a private room and do the "bad" alone or away from adult supervision. Sometimes it meant a place where we could run while wearing our dresses, something that was discouraged since we might sully our nice Sunday clothes. Sometimes it was to eat the snack we were told to not eat, so as not to spoil our dinner. Some of us learn quickly that being good is a show, so you learn to put on a show. But the show is only for them; we learn to protect ourselves from the very people who say they love us, and we love them back.

Las perfectas learn to hide from people they love. They learn to become easily unseen, like furniture, when they are afraid of the adults around them. This will come back to bite them, eventually.

People as individuals and in societies mistreat children in order to fulfill certain needs through them, to project internal conflicts and self-hatreds outward, or to assert themselves when they feel their authority has been questioned. But regardless of their individual motivations, they all rely upon a societal prejudice against children to justify themselves and legitimate their behavior.

—Elisabeth Young-Bruehl

What adults do not seem to want to understand is that while la prima perfecta might fare well in society, it is only in appearance. You have socialized someone into believing that their worth is tied to their ability to have their needs go unmet. Everyone rewards her perfection, there is no doubt about it, yet this is all a dam. Maybe it is even a well-built dam, but one day it will rain and the dam will be tested, and it might endure the first shower, but what about a lifetime of showers? A dam will eventually break, and if it doesn't because it was built on the strongest foundation, it will still crack, and constant maintenance will be required, and then someone has to stop and ask, "What is this dam for anyway? Who is this perfectionism benefitting?"

I have a prima who is perfect. I have a prima who is nice. I have a prima whose word is the Bible. I have a prima I can rely on to never turn her back on me no matter how badly I may treat her. And I value her, I love her. But what about when she meets someone who takes advantage of all those things that we constantly told her made her good and worthy? I wonder where her anger goes because I have never seen it, and we are close. I wonder where she stores that wrath, a wrath we all experience when someone is mean to us and when someone dismisses us, or even when our partners disregard our feelings. Where does that anger get stored, and who will be on the receiving end? Is it her?

I have a prima whom I love and am envious of because I know she makes her parents proud. But at some point, we have to realize that our parents are flawed, and their expectations reflect their contexts and their internalized biases. And at some point, we have to stop aspiring to make them proud even if it goes against our very being. But maybe the point of becoming adults is to make ourselves proud, lest we go put that pressure on our own kids, continuing a cycle of expecting kids to give us that feeling of fulfillment that we should be responsible for giving ourselves.

My perfect prima eventually got a reliable job working at a government agency. She was given a fancy uniform, and she blended in with all the perfect primas. Her dad, who struggles with staying employed, had lost his latest job, and she became the sole financial provider of her household. My perfect prima was so perfect, it made her indispensable. I do not know all the ins and outs, but my perfect prima did get married, which I assume put her family under financial strain again. My guess is that they expected her to never leave.

Being the perfect prima sounds stressful; the weight of people's expectations is suffocating. This is not to say I am against community accountability and everyone pitching in and living in symbiotic relationships. But this is different than that; this is about exploitation and how we socialize girls. Most girls I know were expected to be perfect, good, obedient, seen and not heard. Boys understand that we are being socialized this way, and they think it is normal too. We are all hurt by this.

The best thing that can happen to the oldest prima is that she learns to release all that pressure. It may feel manageable while she is young, but it will all soon become unmanageable. And digging your heels in the sand and demanding that your body manages all the pressure is not going to work out well in the long run. Starting better practices for self-care—and healing wounds created unintentionally by adults who meant well but still fucked up—is how you will get to do this well into your adulthood.

To the family of la prima perfecta, we need to stop rewarding girls for what we deem to be good behavior. We need to stop complimenting parents for what we think we see and start wondering what we do not see. We should stop encouraging people to raise good kids and focus on raising happy kids who know how to name their needs. This is a shift in parenting; it is a shift our parents did not get to carry out with many of us, but even if you think you turned out fine, you probably didn't. We should sit in the discomfort of getting upset at our own parents for having harmed us, intentionally or not. We need to sit with the discomfort that we are actively hurting the children we are tasked with taking care of. And that is not an indictment of whether you are a good parent or a bad parent; that is actually the problem. Everyone makes mistakes, and the value of our character should be in our ability to apologize, reflect, and correct our mistakes—not in our perfectionism and our fight toward never admitting flaws.

To la prima perfecta, you need to understand that your needs must become a priority. If it doesn't feel safe to do that at home, then waiting till you leave is a good-enough strategy. But once you are out, do not compromise your needs for someone else. Leave those old habits behind. It will make for a happier life instead of one that simply looks happy and perfect. And shedding all that fear of being perceived as bad will lead to a longer, healthier life—one you might get to enjoy. I know it sounds easier said than done, but you have to try. If not for the you who is an adult today, then for the younger version of you who deserved better. You can do better by her and help her feel safe. Buy yourself the things you were not allowed to buy. Try new things that you avoided so as not to shame yourself or your family. Push yourself, make yourself uncomfortable, talk back, ask more questions, show disdain, get angry, wear short skirts, and speak up when you see an injustice happening. Becoming the advocate you needed will heal so much within yourself. I promise.

4

WIDOWED TÍA

Relieved of her duties, she finally discovers her freedom.
—Simone de Beauvoir

I SHOULD NOTE THAT I MET MY WIDOWED TÍA AFTER SHE BECAME A widow. I was traveling to a town near hers for work. I had heard a lot about her from other family, and in a spur-of-the-moment decision, I opted to get in touch with her while I happened to be staying close by.

She recommended a restaurant. I arrived first and was ushered to a table. Then I watched her walk in while being greeted like an old friend by the hostess. I instantly recognized her from the family photographs I had seen time and time again. As she was told where I was seated, she gracefully made her way toward me, casually interacting with the restaurant staff along the way. I suddenly realized she had to be a regular.

As she sits down, she shares that this is her favorite restaurant. She points to her regular table, saying with lots of pride that she often comes here with her friends, and they basically shut the place down every time. She has a posse, her confidants. I want to ask her when she met these women, if it was before her husband died or after, but I decide she is too self-aware to miss whatever I may be implying. I might even be unaware of what I'm implying, simply wanting to know but knowing I want to know for a reason, though I do not quite know the full reason.

I want to show her deference. She is my elder, and even as her whimsy makes me forget myself, I manage to remind myself in time. She is a full adult woman, and something about her is telling me that she does not like to be spoken to in roundabout ways—she demands directness.

I think what she makes me feel is adoration with a tinge of jealousy. I am profoundly impressed.

Women are proud of their independence, they finally begin to view the world through their own eyes; they realize they have been duped and mystified their whole lives; now lucid and wary, they often attain a delicious cynicism.

—Simone de Beauvoir

As our dinner progresses, I hear about her very full life. She is a member of a dance group that does traditional dances from her country for big events around the community. She has a group of friends who go golfing and out to brunch together, along with a slew of other regularly planned activities that include only themselves. She is busy. In fact, she is quick to let me know that she herself is surprised she had time to come see me, a little bit tongue-in-cheek.

It is implied that I am lucky to be around her, and I am happy to be reminded of that. I feel lucky, and I welcome her ability to evoke that feeling in the room.

In a youth-obsessed society, we like to think we are gifts to our elders; I have been guilty of this. And yet in those moments with this tía, I find myself longing for her hubris.

My widowed tía is living. I am shocked at my surprise. It is not that I expected her to be in mourning decades after her husband's death. To be frank, I do not know what I expected, but I definitely did not expect her to have such an abundant life. I did not expect to see her so full of life. Maybe that says more about me than her. Maybe that says more about the lies society tells women about life without men. She raised multiple children, and she was a doting wife, as far as anyone was concerned.

I find myself awestruck and covetous. She has something that feels desirable, and I cannot seem to put my finger on it.

Maybe it is that her life excites me; it gives me hope that there is so much more out there for me, for us. She tells me about her friend group and her small community she has since formed. She has four friends who do everything together. They are all around the same age, and all of them are widowed, divorced, or never married. In our chat there is not a mention of a man—Bechdel test approved.

She tells me about her rose garden. Being around her feels thrilling, like stumbling onto a treasure when you were not even told there was one to be found. I had no idea she was this happy. I feel like this should be advertised more: "Widowed older woman comes to life!" We talk for hours, and I feel closer to her than my own mother by the end of our time together. I think it's a sisterly feeling that makes our meeting more intimate; she is family, but in a way she also feels closer than that.

She has nothing but kindness to say about her late husband, but life with him seems too distant. She seems to have come alive alone. I am more intrigued by her current life than anything she can share about her previous life as a wife. The word "wife" feels too empty next to her. Something about saying that, writing that, feels forbidden, and yet it feels true, and to say it differently feels like a lie.

We are socialized to get married and told that being unwed is a reflection of something being wrong with us. So we marry and we do not think twice about it. We feel a sense of duty to our culture, our moms, or even just a duty to ourselves because that is the fate of being a woman: marriage. I think more of us are married out of a sense of responsibility to fulfill our role in society than we are willing to admit or dare to see. I think it feels scary to name that. I dare not say it but I can write it down, and I lie to myself, insisting that I am different. What if I got married out of a deep sense of playing my part, as prescribed through television shows, dolls, mothers, and church communities that often seem to prophesy heterosexual marriages onto girls without asking us what we want. Surely I met someone I could not live without, and that was how it was all meant to be. Surely I am different.

Seeing her come alive is mesmerizing. I wonder if I am asleep, and I don't even know it. I want to ask her about her life; I want to know if she knew she would be this happy. I want to ask her if she knew something was missing while she was married. I want to ask her so many things, but I don't dare bring it all up; I do not want to make this uncomfortable. It is so comforting to be around her, I do not want to spoil it. I hope that by osmosis I can sense her guiding me; I am trying to connect with my body. I want to fill in the blanks, I want to get all the information I can, but I married into her family, and I do not want to insult anyone. I am walking on eggshells while hoping she will take me as her pupil without any words being exchanged.

> *In particular, the woman who "has lived" has a knowledge of a man that no man shares: for she has seen not their public image but the contingent individual that every one of them lets show in the absence of their counterparts; she also knows women, who only show themselves in their spontaneity to other women: she knows what happens behind the scenes.*
>
> —Simone de Beauvoir

This tía can manifest in a dozen iterations. A widow is created by numerous circumstances. I am specifically writing about an elderly widow who has lived a long life with a man who dies at an old age. Her financial circumstances can still differ through this specific scenario. She could be benefitting from a robust life insurance policy; she could just be living life on her terms; she could have lost it all when her husband died, and she is maintained by her children, but this tía looks freer than any woman you know. It is like someone who recently checked off a to-do list, the sigh of relief that comes from doing the thing you needed to get done. Now imagine that feeling embodied. Don't linger on the negative connotations; simply contemplate the release of it all. Imagine an exhale, only incarnated as a tía you have come to love.

This tía has no remorse in showing her happiness. She walks like someone who is at peace with where life has taken her, and with what life has taken *from* her. She has no need to apologize; she did nothing wrong. She is due her independence, and she knows it. We all know it. That is what is so enthralling about watching her: the self-governance of it all.

And do not get me wrong, this tía appropriately mourned her husband, but once she found her rhythm, she became bulletproof. There is nothing anyone can say to change that reality. There is nothing anyone can do to make her look less joyful, and seeing her this happy induces a plethora of feelings I am still sifting through. Come to think of it, I have seldom met a widowed woman who was eternally grieving, but I have met plenty of grieving husbands. My abuelo is one of them, eternally grieving and eternally making a saint of my abuelita. There may be exceptions to the rule, but the rule remains.

I have heard the rumblings of this archetype in tías in unhappy marriages. I cannot count how many times I have heard "mejor sola que mal acompañada" come out of the mouths of my elders and my friends.

The way she talks about going home and eating whatever she wants, and confidently boasts about not having to cook for anyone. When you ask her to make a cultural dish, and she says she's made enough of those for a lifetime, you must let her rest. We all let her rest. You understand what it all means.

> *Her husband was often older than she, she witnesses his decline with silent complacency: it is her revenge; if he dies first, she cheerfully bears the mourning; it has often been observed that men are far more overwhelmed by being widowed late in life: they profit more from marriage than women do, and particularly in their old age, because then the universe is concentrated within the limits of the home; the present does not spill over into the future: it is their wife who assures their monotonous rhythm and reigns over them; when he loses his public functions, man becomes totally useless; woman continues at least to run the home; she is necessary to her husband, whereas he is only a nuisance.*
>
> —Simone de Beauvoir

As a young tía, seeing her this free makes me wonder what I am missing, or rather, what I am carrying with me in order to feel accepted, or to fill a void I was told I possess, without ever wondering if that is even true. I cannot help but widen my gaze around her. I want to memorize her. I look as shocked as I feel seeing someone move without approximately 185–250 pounds weighing her down.

The labor that women are silently carrying out in relationships is heavy, but since it is made invisible, it also goes unseen, sometimes including by us. We all know the additional work we do in relationships, the work our male partners cannot even fully wrap their minds around. Dr. Paul Dolan says women live happier lives without children and a spouse. I think that says a lot about the state of things. I cannot even begin to imagine a world where I don't take on that labor that is often expected from women. I did it growing up for my dad and brother; I abstained, I whispered, and I was taught to keep secrets, to be sneaky about what I needed and wanted.

We have been socialized to be the keepers of grave and serious secrets—especially those that could reveal the everyday strategies of male domination, how male power is enacted and maintained in our private lives.

—bell hooks

It is like we all do this socially mandated checklist out of habit and not with a deep understanding of what we truly may want for ourselves. Maybe she is showing us all what it means to release that, or to have that exorcized from our lives.

My widowed tía speaks clearly about her joy and what it means to feel this independent. No one asks her if she will marry again, and if someone does, they're usually younger and/ or unmarried themselves, and so it is easily dismissed. They do not know yet. She did that already. She does not have to do that again. Banish the thought of taking this grand liberation from her. Her emancipation feels precious to every woman she meets. We are all fascinated.

Your widowed tía might feel different. She may be busy, overworking herself, or living at home with her son, and so she is still under some type of male domination. But she will fight it, in her own way. She may say things like, "No man will ever tell me how to spend my money" in front of the entire family, stopping the men in their tracks. She serves as a warning; she stays in your head, in the back of your throat. She wants you to know she is to be respected. She had her man, and she fed and loved her man, so she is allowed to lean into unruliness. We all understand that she has earned her intoxicating self-governance.

If she slips into resentment, it is because she may have fallen back into being dominated by a man. If she has no residual income left to her, or from her own job, or if she has been cornered into depending on a man again, she will remind you of this offense. She is allowed to be upset that all that labor resulted in continued subjugation.

Sitting and listening to her, you cannot help but take her side. The way she says, "Los hombres no sirven para nada" with the confidence of someone who outlived her husband. You cannot help but wonder how long she has felt this way, how many of the women in your family are currently feeling this way but not saying it, and how long it will take for you to think that way too. You cannot help but wonder . . .

I have this tía who became a widow later in life, and she often says that she has just begun living. She has a fulfilling life, and she acts like she has been waiting her entire life to live this one. And sitting next to her, my appetite begins to grow for her life.

Unironically, this tía will still encourage marriage like an estate planner helping with your end-of-life arrangements. It is like she, too, understands that her unexpected happiness with her life is because death has given her permission to live it. She has earned her place through doing what she was supposed to do: she got married, had children and raised them, and then her husband died. This is her recompense. Maybe that is why she blithely sends you off to your own life of presumed male domination: because she is hoping that you, like her, might outlive him. It all leaves a bad taste in my mouth, the way you're due something only after suffering. It feels like some fucked-up, Christian-centric, rain-before-the-rainbow-type bullshit we have said willingly to make suffering morally superior. The sun is out today, yet we have to earn it?

To the relatives of the widowed tía, fighting against the invisible force of socialization is hard. Insisting on being treated differently is pushing against huge forces that were ingrained in us not just by our parents but by their parents, and their parents' parents, and their parents before them, and the list goes on and on. It is generational work, and it takes time and patience. Maybe that is how we start to become free: when we are given options and not thrust into hoping we outlive someone to earn them. I wish options for us.

To the widowed tía, why start so late? Are we not all due that same happiness? Are we not all deserving of it? Who told you we had to endure to deserve? Who told you this was common sense? Who made it common sense? Have we been stepped on for so long that we think we are born to earn our way out? Who benefits when we believe it all? Complicity is not always an active state; it is in inactivity that we can perpetuate the most harm. If these systems were not meant for our benefit, then maybe the entire industry created to keep women subservient to men and then separated from one another in our individual homes while we labor over these men should be torn down from the ground up.

To the widowed tía, may your joy spark a light within any of us who feel pressured to live life on everyone else's terms but our own. May you watch us not earn self-determination but take it. May we become your liberation, a liberation you never sought but are still owed.

What I have learned while hanging out with my widowed tía is that there is a life without veiled labor. I've learned to start acknowledging when I am doing additional work, and it is not easy. I do not catch it every time; in fact, I think I catch it about 10 percent of the time. I am learning to share parts of me with my partner without the trauma responses that protected me in my patriarchal household. My vulnerability may have been weaponized against me, but that does not mean my partner is the patriarchy. He is a person, and he has the capacity to learn and grow alongside me. I am deserving of joy, and I am deserving of a freer life even in a society that overvalues marriage. You are too.

5

TU TÍA, LA LOCA

*Dominant notions of femininity and the pressure to
conform to those norms can exert a degree of influence on
women's behaviors and consequently their choices.*

—Justin Charlebois

CALLING PEOPLE CRAZY IS NOT ACCEPTABLE. AS WE MOVE TOWARD
destigmatizing mental health struggles, to pejoratively call
someone crazy is to ignore very real systemic problems and
further stigmatize real mental illnesses. I will use this word
in that awful context to frame this tía's reality among her
family because as much as that word is discouraged in specific
spaces, it is still freely used in many communities. This chapter is not about a literal mental illness. This is about someone
who is an intentional agent of chaos, which makes her fodder
for being famously dismissed with a simple four-letter word:
loca. Someone who disrupts the status quo must be shamed
into submission. In this chapter, I am seeking to reclaim
what has been used against me since I was a little girl, and

especially now that I am an adult woman. When that word has been used to sideline you and you somehow keep speaking/writing, you will be amazed at who you will attract.

Tu tía loca is the outcast. The tía who has been rejected. Some say she invites the shunning. I think the shunning is part of the package; being that free means people will try to shackle you into a box any chance they get. She walks into spaces where people snicker at her without doing much to hide it. And she does not appear affected, meaning she does not seek to change how she is treated. Words do not seem to alter her posturing. She allows the snickers to steer her away from people who do not have the range. What she wears is unconventional, and what she says is beyond what some people might consider acceptable.

She is an easy target, someone blatantly disruptive, all while harming no one. But she challenges people's ideas of who they have allowed themselves to become. She actively sits in the discomfort people want to ignore. She feels the discomfort. She does not try to ignore it or soothe it with something that will take her away from feeling it. She has been socialized, just like you, to have similar triggers to things, people, and ideas, but she also insists on finding out where that discomfort comes from and identifying whether she should actually feel what she is feeling. She has questions. She wants to know everything and not necessarily overintellectualize. She taps into her senses, and she challenges herself to learn and push and unlearn.

Under male scrutiny, women will avert their eyes or cast them downward; the female gaze is trained to

*abandon its claim to the sovereign status of seer. The
"nice" girls learns to avoid the bold and unfettered staring of the 'loose' woman who looks at whatever and
whomever she pleases.*

—Sandra Lee Bartky

Once upon a time she may have been closer to being
la prima perfecta. She might have done what she was told
and reshaped herself for approval. She adjusted her expectations to mirror what was expected of her, and she told herself
she had agency, that it was her choice all along. She almost
believed it.

My world crashed and burned one year. My womb could
not hold pregnancies, despite years of being told that my purpose as a woman was to bear children. So I got angry. The
marriage I entered to respectfully leave my parents' home
crumbled. And I began to seethe. I started failing in my
classes at the school I was accepted into after believing the
myth of meritocracy as fact, and then I realized that my hard
work could not compare to white privilege. My blood began to
boil. And then something snapped within me, and I became
what had been scripted for me many years before I decided I
was going to divest from being "good." I became la loca when
I experienced deep heartbreak, and not in a romantic sense,
but in a spiritual sense—a deep break in my spirit. Sometimes
la loca is born out of nurturing parenting and encouragement
to be their own person. And sometimes la loca is made out of
friction and pain, and in the end, the one who emerges is out
for revenge.

You have avenged yourself by having been, through
no fault of your own, a handful to raise and an eternal
thorn in their sides.

                                    —Clarissa Pinkola Estés

Today mi mami says she does not recognize me; she does
not know where I came from, but I look oddly like mi papi's
clone, so birth family deniability is out of the question. However, if she paid any attention to how people spoke about me
growing up, if she dared to put those pieces together, she would
know that I was always this person. A wild woman, someone
who cannot be restrained. As a kid I was called la tocadita al
mal, the black sheep. I was reminded constantly that I was different because I kept insisting and I kept asking for too much.
And one day, I spun myself out of their reach.

Your tía la loca might give off the impression that she is
strong—strong like a dignified woman. In fact, she has a tinge
of it, but dignified women are not impressed by her. Yet they
share more in common than we all dare to admit. The difference is that the dignified woman functions, even as a potential
matriarch, in relationship with the patriarchy—consistently
pushing toward heterosexual marriage and motherhood as the
pinnacle of womanhood. A dignified woman shows restraint,
and la loca runs from it.

This all might make you believe that she is unbelievably
durable. She is not. No one is. She hears all the jokes at her
expense. She hears all the comments. The eye rolls when she
begins to speak make her own skin crawl; it all makes her
want to hide. It has the effect it is meant to have; it is meant to

shame and force someone to bend the knee. But transforming herself into someone more palatable feels like dying, and she rebuffs this because she has witnessed her own lifelessness before, and she does not want to return to that form. That is where she might be seen as strong, but one day she may stop wanting to fight. And she might disappear as you all wish her to, and the ones you will harm along the way are all the primes who are watching these events unfold.

Maybe once they kill her, their bloodstained hands will make them see what they have done to her, to women like her, to women who are difficult. Difficult as in not easily impressed by men; difficult as in having standards; difficult as in hopeful for something better for herself and those around her; difficult as in not easily domesticated; difficult as in she questions tradition; difficult as in she asks more questions than we are prepared to have answers for; difficult as in bigger than life; difficult as in not submissive because she is supposed to be; difficult as in mouthy; difficult as in brilliant as fuck. Imagine wanting to eliminate that and not running to worship the very ground she walks on. Imagine thinking the solution is that she must be controlled.

> *Choosing defiance is a risky tactic unless it is a positively effective action; more time and energy are spent than saved.*
>
> —Simone de Beauvoir

She feels very alone sometimes. The amount of energy put into not getting sucked into gender performance and the male gaze takes up brain space that could be used elsewhere. Yet she is the secret friend with whom you freely share your actual thoughts. She is the person who has been publicly shunned by her church but gets direct messages from the señoras asking her about the things she has said.

She understands the secrecy, but it is wounding. Being nice to those who've been forsaken by others is dangerous. She understands that it is safer for both parties if she stays discarded, even if in their imagination. She is safer there, and so are you; we all know that. And yet she finds herself very alone, often clinging to her few friends who are also shunned in their own communities. Together they get to live a life chosen by themselves, and that is still motivation enough.

I have been banned access to my nieces because I dare to want to hold their dad accountable for the harm he has administered freely toward the women in our family. I have been told I do not watch my tongue around children enough, like I do it by accident. It is not an accident. I speak freely because children should see at least one adult woman living differently, if only to provide a model for them that they deserve to see. They need an alternative to saying less and invisibilizing ourselves for the comfort of men.

Besides, children are not harmed by curse words that are not directed at them. Curse words are just words, expletives. Children are actually harmed by the normalization of diet culture, misogyny, the acceptance of European standards of beauty, and unchecked anger misdirected at them due to unprocessed trauma. Cuss words are nothing in comparison to how we treat them. It is a weird panic focused on the wrong things when what we should be panicking about is how we have normalized adult supremacy and made children suffer through "I tried my best" parental methodology.

Tu tía la loca conjures fear. She touches the red button. She jams her finger into unknown holes. Like a witch, often depicted as living outside the town, in an old shack in the woods, outcast. She is a nightmare to most adults who have chosen a life laid out for them before they were even born. A life that maintains the status quo. A life often copied and pasted from their parents' lives.

The irony is that her life is not safe because they have insisted on the rules applying to us all. If they had to yield, then so should she. She pays for daring to want a different life. People slowly shun her out of public spaces. She exists in the margins, in texts, and in secret phone calls and girls' nights, but not in your wedding parties, baby showers, baptisms, and family reunions. And when she is invited, it is to stand in ridicule for not having done her due diligence and played her role.

In my loca era I was single and over thirty, and I was treated like a threat, like I was there to steal someone's man. As if any man is worth that effort and energy. I have found that marriage to a man has pacified the indignation; the label of loca is less easily brandished. In another lifetime I am sure I would have been burned at the stake. In this lifetime, I could have been killed at some club or even found dead after one of my many one-night stands. I think ultimately, my marriage has been what has made me acceptable. Not my partner, specifically, but the fact that I am married to a cis hetero man. The legitimacy that a man offers me is still of value, even as much as we like to think of ourselves as beyond that. Other facts come into play also, but ultimately, between husbands I experienced a fear-binding existence because being la tía loca who is single was dangerous, and my entire body sensed it. That thought haunts me. The idea that a heterosexual relationship is my "saving grace" sends shivers down my spine.

If tu tía loca is single or in a non-heterosexual relationship, trust that she is told about the prayers for her salvation—often. If she is childless and single, she is considered a pariah, and she is treated as such. How dare she take up so much space when she has done none of the items on her female-assigned checklist? How dare she continue to insist that she matters? How dare she not show misery for her misfortune of not having been chosen?

> *If a woman takes a stand politically, socially, spiritually, familially, environmentally, if she points out that some particular emperor has no clothes, or if she speaks for those who are hurt or who are without voice, too often her motives are examined to see if she has "gone wild," that is, crazy.*
>
> —Clarissa Pinkola Estés

Being la tía loca means a lack of true connection in public spaces with women who perform a heteronormative femininity. Women claim their distance from your tía loca, almost as though on autopilot, out of fear of being lumped alongside her. She makes people afraid, and in turn she feels that fear. That fear pushes her; it pushes her to follow the rules in public to have access to her family. Everything in her body rejects this new path she is forging. She has years of socialization under her belt telling her she is wrong for doing anything other than what she was taught.

She knows what is expected of her because of her gender. She has been taught how to behave like a "good woman" her entire life, and it might still be second nature. Tu tía la loca might experience her own body trying to push her toward what she has known. She might experience hives or other similar responses when she behaves in ways that go against what she has been told is "proper."

The path to embracing the chaos of being the titular crazy tía is little-known, and it is unpaved or barely paved. Choosing to feel crazy, or to be made to feel crazy, is harder than words can fully describe. Tu tía loca feels everything—her joints ache, her skin wants to run away from her bones, and her body goes into panic mode. She feels profoundly and dangerously. Tu tía loca is hurting because when she speaks, she is shunned at best and killed off by society at worst.

But she defies everything anyway, and that is precisely why it is lunacy. She is fighting years of girl-rearing, but one day there will be more defiant years under her belt than programmed ones, and it will all feel easier. It has to feel easier. At some point, the reward of true freedom outweighs the burden of burning bridges that lead to respectable womanhood. She cannot imagine ever finding happiness being who she is supposed to be instead of becoming lo que le dé la regalada gana.

She cannot fit without also dying.

                      —Clarissa Pinkola Estés

To the tía loca, do not let their world become your preoccupation. Living should be your preoccupation. You have figured out how to live a dream many of the women in your family have only ever imagined, and it is important that you live that life you have so fearlessly fought to live. Take vacations, smoke that weed, take that edible on a Monday at 2:00 p.m., go to rallies, join labor movements, never step foot into a church and say it is because you might melt if you do enter a sanctuary, laugh with strangers, read books you would never pick up, surprise yourself, surpass yourself. Do the things you know you would not be able to do if you lived another life, a life that requires self-abnegation. So lean into doing everything your heart desires, and find what you enjoy in those moments. At first, it will feel like live-action role-playing another life, maybe even the life of a man. But eventually it will feel natural, and it will be your life to live. And do not apologize for living that life.

Furthermore, in your abundance of time and energy, try to help free others.

Your real job is that if you are free, you need to free somebody else. If you have some power, then your job is to empower somebody else. This is not just a grab-bag candy game.

                      —Toni Morrison

To the family of tu tía loca, try to keep her around. And when you think you are done trying because she has pushed your buttons one too many times, try again. Because by her existing as she does, she is creating a universe of options for everyone who witnesses her. By existing, and being allowed to exist, she is showing a newer generation what is possible and what can be. If the good outweighs the physical discomfort her unquestioned presence creates, keep her around, and learn to sit in uncomfortable feelings—it is healthy to learn to sit with feelings we cannot name. May those feelings open you up to something else within yourself. You might begin to think la tía loca is not crazy because she feels familiar to you, and reading this may feel like too eerie a monologue. If she feels like an invitation, I dare you to RSVP.

She is crazy. She sees the order of things as created for us through heteronormativity, patriarchy, racism, and the status quo, and she wants to unbalance it. She needs to disturb it to not feel crazy. You see what is wrong too. You want it gone too. But it can feel threatening to disturb this order of things, what has been set in stone, so encourage those who do take the risks that are necessary to really change things.

6

THE TÍA WHO SEES FANTASMAS

To speak of the spiritual with respect to the cultural practices of politically disempowered communities, particularly the work of women, is perhaps even more fraught with dangers.

—Laura E. Pérez

THIS PARTICULAR TÍA, AS I HAVE SEEN AND EXPERIENCED HER, VARIES. And while in previous chapters I have conflated various people into one archetype, this one requires me to explain the range in which this tía may present herself. The main reason for doing this is because I come from women who see ghosts, and it is normal to say so within my family. There are no weird glances, there are no surprises, and there is no mockery involved when seeing ghosts is par for the course.

The spirit world in Latin American households feels closer than it does in upper-middle-class white American households. This is a great example of IYKYK (if you know, you know), and to attempt to fully convince anyone who does not "get it" feels like labor I am not willing to take on. I make that note because I now live around upper-middle-class white American people, and I do not hear their ghost stories... ever. And it is a point of contention how often sharing my own experiences with the supernatural makes people outside my communities visibly uncomfortable—unless they, too, are from a BIPOC low-income household.

Meanwhile, I grew up hearing ghost stories from the adults in my life very regularly. This was not meant to scare me or any of the children who were in the room when these stories were shared. These moments when everyone shared their ghost stories were comforting. Having adults try to put words to the unexplained felt important in my formation. To have the unexplained spoken into existence was part of my education.

I grew up with fables, too, these common stories told generation upon generation to children. I was told about La Llorona and the Grim Reaper. I knew the difference between a fable that was meant to teach me something about staying out of the house past daylight and stories about our families' encounters. And sometimes they crossed over too. Like the time my dad went to a rural town in Colombia and saw the silhouette of the Grim Reaper outside his window, a story that was corroborated by the other men who were with him that night. They all laughed about having to hold their pee because the outhouse was too far away for any of them to dare make the walk after that apparition.

I grew up hearing firsthand ghost encounters from family members. That is what I mean when I say that the spirit world in Latin American households feels close. Everyone has a story, and if you do not have a story, you are often left out of a very crucial part of our lives. These moments of sharing ghost stories during a citywide blackout were my absolute favorite, most cherished moments with my family. So with that starting point, and understanding that growing up hearing about ghost encounters is the baseline of common knowledge in our communities, there needs to be an understanding of the tías who see ghosts and how they feel. Because while everyone in my family, regardless of gender, has these stories, the women's encounters were usually the most captivating. I do not know if it is because storytelling is a more gender-specific way of rearing girls, or if the television made for women tends to be story-centric, or if it's a combination of a lot of factors. But the women in my family tend to be more curious about the spirit realm and speak of it more freely than the men.

Today, we grapple with our need to thoroughly understand who we are—gifted human beings—and to believe in our gifts, talents, our worthiness and beauty, while having to survive within the construct of a world antithetical to our intuition and knowledge regarding life's meaning.

—Ana Castillo

When we reflect on our ghost encounters as a family unit, it is usually in the past tense. But I have one tía who shares her encounters with you as they are happening right before her very eyes, and only to her, even as you stand beside her. For this, she exists in the margins of what is possible, and many people dismiss her or explain her away.

This tía may go years without seeing a ghost, but when she does see something supernatural, her eyes will wander in a room, and sometimes she will speak to the apparition. Other times she will describe what the apparition is doing, and you can hear a pin drop after she is done speaking. I have been escorted out of the room during these instances by another tía. I have heard other women in my family, who do believe that spirits visit us, whisper about this tía. They call her attention-seeking. There is something disturbing about someone seeing something you cannot see while you are sharing the same space. I think it scares them; I know it scared me. That level of connectedness is scary because we cannot fathom that it could possibly be real, that it could possibly be true, that we could possibly be chosen in that way.

In my household, where ghosts are normal, mental health problems are often not seen as normal or normalized. In my family, we do not talk about mental health problems. In my family, we seek the spirit world to heal us from mental health problems through prayers and the laying of hands. The spirit realm becomes all-encompassing, to explore the unexplained and explain the unexplained.

I come from a family in which I am the first to seek therapy. I have also had encounters with ghosts. I do not think those two things are necessarily related, but I am also not entirely sure they aren't. My mental health struggles are closely related to systemic oppression, and my debilitating anxiety stems from external messaging around my worthiness because I am not white and a man living in a world that rewards white men for existing. So I struggle with feeling like I should eliminate myself because I feel my outsider status in heightened ways on a daily basis. My generational trauma I have been able to name comes from national traumas that wounded my family and their ability to feel safe, and thus I deal with little things like perfectionism and disguising pain with bravado to not appear weak and prey-like. And in my lowest mental health moments, I have been more open to the supernatural. I encountered the ghost who haunts my current home when I was still figuring out if I was safe in my relationship with the person who also shares that home with me. This heightened awareness made me susceptible to paranoia, and that is when I first met my ghost roommate.

In haunting, organized forces and systemic structures that appear removed from us make their impact felt in everyday life in a way that confounds our analytic separations and confounds the social separations themselves.
—Avery F. Gordon

I am someone who believes that trying to find the words to explain something when we may lack the vocabulary to do so is unwise. And yet these are the things I have seen as they were manifesting themselves in my family. I hesitate to explain away this tía in the same way that words like "crazy" have historically been used to silence women. I do not want to be misunderstood as armchair diagnosing her with a mental illness she may or may not have. She may be seeing what she says she is seeing; I cannot prove or disprove that.

The tía who is hypersensitive to the spirit realm expresses that instinct in a way that is a bit different than what is socially expected or practiced. This tía is very much a type of tía that I will not erase simply because it makes people uncomfortable. She is part of this story as much as the tías who see ghosts and know when it is socially acceptable to share those stories.

I have another tía who speaks of being visited by dead ancestors. This tía does not live extensive alternate lives with these apparitions; rather, they will specifically visit her when they die. This tía, as I know her, lives in the USA, and distance has meant she was not able to see her own mother before she died. But she did sense her when she passed.

I think that these farewells, these despedidas from ancestors, are pivotal for a tía who lives so far from her roots. Maybe it is the ancestors understanding that borders were created to divide us and keep us fractured, so they are tending to the wounds that borders create. This tía had no comfort when distance robbed her of her chance to hug a loved one for the last time, and these apparitions are sacred to her. These apparitions soothe where borders traumatize. This tía always promises to come visit you when she dies. This tía's eyes show sadness in disconnection but gratitude for what she did receive. I have tenderness for her because I have seen this tía cry many tears, never daring to rob her of her goodbyes with an explanation. If she said it happened, it happened; she is given space to say her despedidas, and that is more important to any interpretation.

Truth is a subtle shifting entity not simply because phi-
losophy says so or because evidentiary rules of validation
are always inadequate, but because the very nature of
the things whose truth is sought possesses these qualities.
—Avery F. Gordon

I have another tía who has a slew of stories of hearing noises and feeling guided by her ancestors. This tía often looks to signs around her. She is into astrology or numerology. This tía loves tarot and readings and stays connected to the spirit world through other non-traditional spiritualities. Some people find one religious practice that suits their needs and commit, but this tía finds little comfort in rigidity. Instead, this tía loves the complexity and vastness of not knowing and chipping away at the unexplained. This tía does not judge because she is often judged. This tía looks at you as you search for what is unsaid because she knows how dogmatic religions can override natural instincts. This tía is softhearted, and she is generous when you ask her questions. She hates labels and especially hates boxes. Ask her a question and she will give you so many answers you will begin to wonder what you asked to begin with. Gentle guidance from the ancestors feels important to this tía. She may dabble in understanding the spirit world, or she may find herself to be an expert. Either way, listen to her.

This tía is also the one with warnings. This tía dreams that your long-awaited trip is going to turn into a tragedy and begs you to take another train/flight/boat. This tía gets a feeling about people; she warns you to dump your new novio because she can just tell he is going to harm you in some way. This tía gets sick to her stomach and does not know why but then gets a phone call that someone was in a wreck, and she is quick to connect the two instances. It is unsettling to hear your tía got a bad feeling about something because having to explain this to anyone outside your family is hard to do. But these premonitions have been spot-on at one point or another, and so when she speaks these things into a room, people pause and rethink what they had initially considered to be a good decision. I have not changed a flight before, but I have ended a relationship based on the constant warnings from this tía.

It is spiritual wisdom that has reemerged over the last fifty years as we advance in our efforts to decolonize our lives, our minds, our spirits, our bodies.
—Lara Medina and Martha R. Gonzales

I have many tías who all have their own stories with ghosts but do not actively seek to see or sense anything. They are the ones who believe in not conjuring things you cannot understand. They chalk it up to having respect for the dead; they say that they don't dabble in that stuff because they respect the afterlife. These tías do not enjoy seeking ghost stories.

Ghost stories happen to them, and they are very clear about the encounters they have had. They happily listen to and believe in ghost encounters others have had because of their own experiences. But these tías have no interest in long-term encounters with the afterlife. There is even fear for them surrounding the unknown elements of ghost encounters. These tías believe that spirits can also be evil, and that scares them. They are the tías who tell you not to play with Ouija boards. They tell you not to play with candle flames and ask questions to an empty room. They will tell you to stay away from things you cannot understand; there is no need to abrir puertas to things you are not sure are connected to good spirits. They are the ones who bid us all to remain vigilant and aware.

The cautious tías practice a Judeo-Christian religion that has introduced concepts like Satan to them. Because Satan is God's enemy, they stay alert. Also, they know that too much of a spirituality that is disallowed by their church is dangerous. They know when to share their stories, and to whom. They also know when not to share their stories. And they know when a spirit is good or bad based on a Christian sense of good and evil. They find comfort in their sense of knowing, and it keeps them from venturing anywhere that may feel too disruptive to their regular lives. They are also quick to label exploration of the spirit realm as demonic. They have rigid rules for engaging in nonrigid things like the supernatural. But it makes them feel safe, and it helps it stay fun, which is important to them.

Power can be invisible, it can be fantastic, it can be dull and routine. It can be obvious, it can reach you by the baton of the police, it can speak the language of your

thoughts and desires. It can feel like remote control, it can
exhilarate like liberation, it can travel through time,
and it can drown you in the present.

—Avery F. Gordon

When I first realized that not all cultures have this open dialogue about fantasmas, I was well into adulthood. For a long time, I thought that when people dismissed ghosts as not real, it was just to seem smarter, less illogical—as if logic functions that neatly.

I have been raised in Latine neighborhoods and around Latine people. Whenever someone from my context questioned the validity of ghosts, which did not occur often, I thought that they were just trying to be cool. They were trying to fit in with a white American perception of the world, making themselves feel better by making fun of something that felt so obviously factual for the sake of being contrarian and feeling superior. I have done that; I have denied facts and lived experiences for the sake of citations because it was what I was told was preferred, and I knew to mirror that even when I did not believe it. I knew that thinking got me good grades, and so I behaved accordingly. But it never completely dawned on me that people suppress that stuff to such an extent that they do not believe in it, their kids do not believe in it, and their kids' kids do not believe in it. It never dawned on me that somewhere along their generations, it became so unexplainable that it was untrue. Today I understand that assimilation takes our mother tongues, our family recipes, and our cultural cues, but it also robs us of our ancestral knowledge. Now I understand the enormity of what they were missing. I am reminded of that when I inhabit white spaces and I receive concerned looks when I speak about my encounters with the supernatural as natural happenstances. White Americans will shame you into assimilation, and they will do that even in the most progressive of spaces.

I was floored to hear that some people have not heard their parents tell of a single personal encounter with ghosts. I am still floored to hear some people express zero interest in their family's supernatural encounters, and to hear that they have never even asked those questions. When I finally met someone who just wanted nothing to do with the conversation, I began to realize that the supernatural was not fact for them. That reality still burns—the idea that someone has lived an entire life missing out on something so integral to human development as the thrill of knowing we do not know everything. That makes me feel sorry for them. Because what my ghost-sharing gatherings with family taught me was so much more than ghost stories.

What those moments taught me was how to tell good stories, better than any teacher I had ever could. Those moments taught me how to make people laugh with a story, how to make people scared with a story, and how to bring the right amount of details to a storytelling circle. It meshed fantasy, magic, and first-person narratives into one big and exciting moment of seeing your family play together. It felt crucial to watch adults play through storytelling. It helped develop and preserve parts of my memories for stories I knew I would later share with my family. It helped me imagine a life bigger and more abundant than the lives we were living, but one that could be a reality because if the supernatural is possible, so is the ability to outlive poverty and all the systems meant to kill you. If you can outlive death, you can never be forgotten.

Furthermore, it taught me to see value in the skill of oral storytelling. It taught me that my family members who all see ghosts are magic. And through my tías who saw ghosts, I saw women play with men and beat them at it. The tías in my family would weave their ghost encounters into epics, and I still remember their stories like it was yesterday.

To the family surrounding a ghost-seeing tía, if you are a doubter, keep that to yourself. You do not know what you're extinguishing when you minimize someone's reality. Some people go to work every day from nine to five and get two weeks off and call that thriving. Telling people their lives are lies helps no one feel better about their circumstances. Be gentle with how you speak to those of us who are trying to keep some power alive within ourselves.

Also, lean into it. If you are a spectator in these exchanges but have never indulged in sharing your own stories, dare to speak your encounter to the room. My partner spent six years of our relationship telling me he did not believe in ghosts, and then one day he shared his own ghost story of when he was just a boy, and it bonded us. I felt so close to him. He shared something that could have been (and probably was) weaponized against his intelligence, and we held it. It is important to get involved and to allow that play to exist in family dynamics. Do not let linear logic rob you of the ability to joyfully explore other ways of thinking.

To the tía who sees ghosts, keep sharing your stories. Keep daring to see everything a little bit clearer. Keep staying open to the possibilities. Do not let the voices that devalue female spirituality keep you from dreaming and experiencing life outside the confines of normalcy. And do not feel trapped into believing that logical thinking can only be linear by trying to explain yourself to anyone—you are above it all. We are past explaining ourselves. You have been touched by something we cannot explain. In you doing what you should be doing, you make us brave. I push back against the silencing that occurs around the supernatural all the time because I want to live in a world where things do not always make sense. We are not meant to be the same, so why bother trying to emulate the norm when being irregular is much more fun?

7

STREET-SMART PRIMA

Girls performed different versions of femininity that were integrally linked to and inseparable from their class and racial/ethnic performances.

—Julie Bettie

WHEN MI ABUELITA CÁNDIDA WAS DYING, MY PARENTS WERE ABLE TO fly into Nicaragua. However, because it was so sudden, they could afford only their own flights, so my siblings and I were unable to go. But mi mami tells this story about my street-smart prima that brings me peace knowing she was around during those sad times.

By the time my parents arrived in Nicaragua, my dad's siblings had already taken my abuelita to the hospital, and moving her was not an option. She was dwindling fast. Because I do not come from a family of means, the hospital they chose was the best option they had for her care. And as a result, she was at a hospital where they did not provide sheets, pillows, or even bathrooms, just bedpans, and no one was bathing her. Taking her there did not feel like the solution that everyone thought it would be, and in some ways, she would have been better off at home. Nicaragua is a very poor country, and us living paycheck to paycheck in the USA meant that my US-based parents did not have money saved for a rainy day, and everyone just had to accept what was happening. Overall, the conditions were not what anyone would want for their dying mom, wife, sister, or grandmother. Only two people were allowed into her hospital room at a time.

> *So, if women must, they will paint blue sky on jail walls. If the skeins are burnt, they will spin more. If the harvest is destroyed they will sow more immediately. Women will draw doors where there are none, and open them and pass through into new ways and new lives. Because the wild nature persists and prevails, women persist and prevail.*
> —Clarissa Pinkola Estés

As mi mami tells it, my street-smart prima hit the ground running. She befriended the staff at the hospital just by adjusting and adapting. She gained the favor of the cleaning staff by doing the same thing. From the people who cleaned the bathrooms to the nurses, she began to know them all by name. The emotional labor it must have taken to have conversations with these people is unimaginable. She was working at a call center at the time, and she would make an effort to bring food for the entire hospital staff on my grandmother's floor. Nothing fancy, just sandwiches and tajadas con queso. This prima knew that her abuelita's end-of-life days depended on her ability to read a situation. She tackled it with every ounce in her body. Failure was not an option.

Hospital rules said that visitors were not even allowed to stay with her overnight, even though the staff knew full well she needed help even just to use the bedpan. The situation was distressing for everyone involved, and many of my grandmother's children stayed away because it was difficult to see their mother in such distress. Confronting the reality of the situation felt too hard.

But my street-smart prima did not stay away. Soon enough, the staff managed to get mi abuelita clean bedsheets and pillows, and the cleaning staff would leave a door open for our family to sneak into the hospital after hours and keep her company. Most of the wives of my grandmother's sons took shifts to be present and help clean her up.

Because the hospital staff had grown fond of my street-smart prima, we were given special treatment. Soon enough, the hospital staff was checking in on my abuelita and asking us what our family needed. Their resources were also limited, and they were severely overworked, but my street-smart prima was able to obtain the bare minimum everyone needed to make my abuelita's last days less uncomfortable. Because of her valiant labor, the hospital staff allowed everyone in my family to say their goodbyes to my abuelita in a large group and past the allotted time for visitors. That is how life goes when you are with my street-smart prima; things align because she figures out how to make them align.

Among wolves, no matter how sick, no matter how cornered, no matter how alone, afraid, or weakened, the wolf will continue. She will lope even with a broken leg. She will go near others seeking the protection of the pack. She will strenuously outwait, outwit, outrun, and outlast whatever is bedeviling her. She will put her all into taking breath after breath. She will drag herself, if necessary, just like the duckling, from place to place, till she finds a good place, a healing place, a place for thriving.

—Clarissa Pinkola Estés

I deeply admire women who are unwilling to let anything stop them. I admire women who are sharp. Sharp enough to know better, sharp enough to not be fooled, sharp enough to anticipate. That sharpness is something that is learned through an abundance of experiences that teach you to stay alert. My street-smart prima feels alert but not paranoid. She is always ready to spring into action but is not tense; or rather, she knows to hide any signs of what could be perceived as defenselessness.

I have watched my street-smart prima develop right before my eyes since she is younger than me by two years. We grew up together, though admittedly I was always closer to her older sister since our birthdays were just one day apart. Also, her sister is quieter and less likely to take up space, which can give people like me more permission to be louder and take up more space. My street-smart prima and her sister are also very close; I think it is for the same reasons.

With every visit to Nicaragua, my street-smart prima only got sharper. Mi mami has this compliment she brandishes specifically for this prima. It is a compliment when she says it, but in a culture that prefers women to be soft and docile, it is often misinterpreted as an insult. Mi mami calls this prima "viva." To be viva is to be alive, in the literal sense. To be alive is to live with your eyes wide open. To be aware of various factors and have the ability to adjust quickly. When you grow up poor, to be viva is to survive. Someone who is viva is always going to be okay, maybe even better than okay, and that is valuable.

I once tweeted, "I love it when women are vivas." And the responses I received were interesting. Some people attempted to correct me into believing that a woman who is viva is actually someone we should reject. Again, being this sharp is dangerous to people who will try to manipulate you or your loved ones. To be prickly is to be ready to pounce, always on the defensive; people like that will not be easily taken advantage of, and if you are on the side of the ones who are taking advantage, then yes, someone who is viva is someone to be managed, controlled, tamed, and stifled. A mujer being called viva as a celebration turns the status quo on its head, and to rebuff that means that in your communities, women are not allowed to do that, even when necessary.

Someone who is viva will circumvent every narrow-minded perception of her and adjust before you even realize she's outsmarting you. I have seen it happen. The ease and quick shifts that my street-smart prima exhibits, such as adjusting her posture and tone to fit a person or a space, that shit is fascinating to watch. I remember her taking me to a tattoo parlor and adjusting her look while in the car on our way there, untucking her tank top and tussling her short, jet-black hair. I saw her adapt and shift to fit a space while I sat there not touching an inch of myself, wondering where I would even begin but knowing I was supposed to learn something from that scenario. By switching she teaches others to adjust without saying a fucking word. This cousin has taught me to assess people and then make calculated decisions based on what I want and what I need. She understands normative value systems, value systems by class, and value systems of older, dignified señoras—the holy trinity of understanding. It is like she has a third eye that perceives differently because she is truly seeing things for what they are and what they intend to do.

Whenever I am with this prima, it feels like I am safe. This prima has a bolder personality that is funnier, louder, but she's also quieter, meeker, and respectful of her elders when she knows she must be. She is respected because she understands traditions and codes of performance and subverts it all when she is safe and in private. She does the dance we are supposed to do, but she does it better than anyone I know. And you can see it in her eyes that she knows exactly what she is doing and why she must. There is almost a joy in it for her. Her eyes come alive when she has to activate that within herself; she opens them wider like she is engaging her "on" setting.

She grew up like we all did in Nicaragua, churched and hyperconservative. And there is something about a lot of churched women; we can sometimes look like injured animals. We are too shy sometimes, much to our own demise. We lack conviction unless it is about God and what the Bible says about our roles as mothers and wives. And we can avoid saying too much, lest we say the wrong thing. It is a weird burden because churched women are supposed to reflect the perfect, purely chaste example of Christianity; and all of that is felt, but oftentimes it is all too hard to name, and even harder to live. Seeing someone who is so alive, not allowing shame to tame her... it is hypnotic.

Within Latina cultures, stereotypes of marianismo (like the Virgin Mary) require martyrdom and quiet suffering rather than anger.

—Sharon Lamb

The street-smart prima grew up in this environment like we all did, but she managed to not let it steal important parts of who she is today. Or she allowed the information she received to inform the strategy she developed for outsmarting it. Even as I see parts of her in myself, there are parts of me that have been simmered down to a slow burn.

In some ways, I am the street-smart prima in the USA. I grew up here and had to adjust and learn codes of ethics and modes of behavior that applied to certain situations and helped me get by. The fact that I am where I am today writing this book for y'all is not a product of family wealth or connections. It is also not because I had great mentors who took care of me while I was in high school. My IQ is not impressive by any means. My ability to be here is because I outsmarted people and systems, I was in the right place at the right time, and I kept pushing. Failure was not an option. And yet, I fight myself all the time and feel shame for saying too much and pushing too far. Everything in our culture wants us, girls and women, to be tame and stay small. Bigness is considered a threat, and threats are quickly shamed back into smallness—these are the cycles of our lives. These are the internal battles—our street-smart battles, on a larger scale—where much more feels at stake.

The street-smart prima could make friends with a wall! She is vibrant and funny. She can connect with anyone anywhere. She is the prima who always knows someone, who knows someone, who knows someone. She knows how people like to be spoken to based on class, gender, race, title, etc. and uses it to her advantage like no other. Unlike the perfect prima, she knows to turn it off. She knows that what this performance gets her is the goal, but she does not kill off parts of herself in the long term for any of it. She does not pretend to come from any other situation to be read differently. Rather, she moves past it and works with the lines as they exist. She is not here to dismantle anything; she is here to make shit happen, and she does.

It is magnetic to watch her. She never makes people feel less-than, and she never speaks down to people. She looks everyone in the eyes. She will speak to someone who is experiencing homelessness like she will speak to a doctor. And she holds people with power to a higher standard, expecting them to be twice as nice and twice as welcoming—and when she is disappointed, as she often is, she has no problem telling someone that their shit stinks like everyone else's. And somehow, some way, she ends up making friends with whomever she just destroyed verbally because she is seldom wrong. People should treat people as they want to be treated, and everyone seems to hear that when she says it. You cannot help but take her side.

Whenever someone she knows is going through a tough time, financially or otherwise, she is the one who will call and plead their case. She does not let pride stop her from helping others. When my uncle got Covid-19 and was hospitalized, he was refusing to call my dad for any help. He did not want to be an inconvenience. My dad helps his siblings every chance he gets, and in this case his younger brother felt like my dad was already doing more than expected. It was this cousin who picked up the phone and called my dad. My dad then called a few family friends, and they were able to get my uncle back home and cared for by another family friend and doctor. My uncle was able to make a full recovery. This prima did that. She did what others will not do or are too ashamed to do. Her convictions are strong; family is everything.

This prima is also the first one to think of something that will get us all into some sort of trouble, and then somehow, because everyone loves her, nobody will be upset to discover whatever mischievous thing we have done.

My prima is so sturdy in her convictions and in herself that even the adults in our lives trust that we are safe with her. I have this prima who everyone thinks is the tough one, the one who cannot get hurt, the one who will never be taken advantage of, and we all rely on her to be that steady ocean in our lives. Powerful and constant, and always giving more to us than we give to her. I feel close to this prima. I know so much about how she became this way, and there is so much I do not know because being the strong one often means curbing your own appetite, curbing your own needs, to save the family. Being the street-smart prima has a cost, often paid without much instruction, warning, or consent. But it changes the ways you move through spaces, and it also alters how the world treats you because of how you have come to navigate the world.

Learning to outsmart and outlast means stretching yourself past limits that may have been painful to learn. Social skills that are admired, like hers, are often garnered through tears and torment. This world will break your heart before you figure out how to survive it.

> *A list of instructions to girls includes: talk to her, don't yell, sit here, pick that up, be careful, be gentle, give it to me, put it down there. Girls may have received fewer bodily instructions than did boys, but they received more directive ones. This gender difference leaves boys a larger range of possibilities of what they might choose to do with their bodies…whereas girls were directed toward a defined set of options.*
>
> —Karin A. Martin

If you have a street-smart prima, you know that her presence in your family is currency. If you have a street-smart prima, you love the shit out of her, and so does everyone else. She can do no wrong, regardless of how she gets stuff done. In contexts where surviving is worth everything, what is lost? To the family of the street-smart prima, lean in and learn more about what she is doing, and help. Rather than making her indispensable, seek to emulate her. She cannot always be our saving grace, like the matriarch, and we cannot sit back and let her take on these giant tasks and think that it will not affect her in the long term.

The anguish of becoming the street-smart prima is unspoken. Kids should not have to learn how to read adults to adjust and accommodate. That is where those skills stem from—households with fickle parents who, depending on the day, could rain hell on your life if you were not careful. Those skills come from survival. Those skills come from dark places, and yes, they can reap wonderful benefits as we move through the world. And those benefits can be praised, but we cannot ignore what is really happening.

I clench my jaw subconsciously. I hold my tension in my body when I enter new situations and meet new people because being this alive and this aware takes a lot of energy. I carry a huge knot in the back of my neck from bracing my shoulders whenever I am performing to get what I need to get on any given day. I brace myself for life because life does not just happen to me, I make it happen. The toll it has taken on my body means that I also pay a high price to heal. Attempting to heal while living in a society that you must continue to outsmart—that is a task more difficult than anyone can imagine unless you know these experiences in your gut too.

My street-smart prima, she lives in another country now. She married, and I do not hear much from her. We have grown distant; in our busyness we have lost track of each other. And yet I always assure myself that she is going to be okay, in the same way I know mi mami thinks that I am going to be okay. The strong ones are always okay, but are we? We are alive, and we are living with an abundance of information to help us outsmart situations, but are we okay? Am I okay?

I have developed a few autoimmune disorders, my stress levels are through the roof, and it reflects in my blood pressure. Am I okay?

These are new questions I have begun to pose to myself. After the movie *Encanto* came out, it took me a bit to figure out why I kept crying whenever I saw Luisa Madrigal. Luisa is depicted as the strong one. Physically, she can carry the whole town on her back. Luisa's storyline is about the pressure she feels to be that and the harm it does to her. I am not physically strong, but my mental fortitude is unmatched. In fact, only my street-smart prima knows what it is like, and yet we both forge on. We are the same but different. Cut from the same cloth but living two separate realities.

To the family of the street-smart prima, to those who benefit from resilience and strength, I implore y'all to investigate that more. And I understand—many of us are still in situations that require our resilience and our strength. I understand that investigating all of that may not be useful when we very much just want to celebrate the skills that continue to work for us. We have chiseled ourselves to perfection, to protect ourselves and our families.

I have this prima who I know I cannot replace. I have this prima who makes me feel invincible while being the actual invincible one, and I wonder if there is anyone making her feel how she makes others feel.

To the street-smart prima, who will advocate for you when you are not able? Are these the seeds you are planting? If so, know that you will be taken care of regardless of what gifts you bring or do not bring to the table. To the street-smart prima, learn to let your sisters take the lead; they might surprise you. To the street-smart prima, I wish you happiness beyond your worth being tied to your resilience. To the street-smart prima, I wish for you to have someone you can rely on. I hope you find that not in a husband but in a partner. You need an equal. You do not need another person to save; you need someone who will be there for you and willing to go above and beyond what is expected. I hope you find the strength to ask more of your sisters. The true strength here is in your ability to make yourself replaceable so that you can begin to rest. From years of being the strong ones, I wish rest for us.

8

DIGNIFIED TÍA

Girl children who display a strong instinctive nature often experience significant suffering in early life. From the time they are babies, they are taken captive, domesticated, told they are wrongheaded and improper.

—Clarissa Pinkola Estés

I WAS RAISED BY THIS ARCHETYPE. I KNOW IT WELL. SHE IS THE OLDEST daughter, the one who did it first, the one who figured things out for everyone else. She is the house manager. As the oldest daughter in my own household, she taught me everything I know about being tough. The pipeline from perfect prima, to dignified tía, to matriarch is as clear as day.

The dignified tía is a matriarch in the making, or might already be a matriarch. Not all women become a matriarch, as a matriarch requires access to borrowed power, which she wields over her family unit. This power trumps her partner's. The type of moral superiority that makes the backbone of a dignified tía is necessary for the matriarch role, wherein she will often become the decision-maker in many family disputes. Another aspect of this tía is that while her children grew up with this dignified tía in all her dignified glory, her grandchildren often soften the edges of this archetype, really rounding out this tía.

I have met a few dignified tías in my life, and they all have that same look. There is neither a smile in their eyes nor on their faces. They are very polite but short in their exchanges. They are measuring you, evaluating. They are looking at the way you speak to people depending on age; they are looking to see where you put your hands; they are asking you about your friends to measure your own trustworthiness. They are interrogating who you are based on how you behave.

This tía consistently moves with an air of pride mixed with rage. Imagine growing up as a formidable woman in a society and culture that prefers women to submit, and then imagine what that does to this formidable woman. Don't imagine her rich and white and fragile; imagine her working-class with thick, wavy hair and a serious face that says, "Fuck around and find out," and imagine her speaking a language we do not deem interesting or sexy. Imagine her looking like the help. Because how we see her within our family, and how the world sees her, is different.

I have seen it; I have seen these women bend and then learn to get up anyway. When they get up, they hold their heads so high so that no one will ever step on them again. And yet, they get their knees taken out from under them, again and again, and they learn to get up and reposition themselves to withstand more. No one held their hand, so they learned to help themselves. They were expected to take it all, by their families and by this world.

As a result of all that, she is sometimes quick to brandish advice and try to help others with the knowledge she has learned along the way, even when you are not asking for any advice.

These are the tías who will overstep out of the best intentions. They are the wise ones, the ones who think they have suffered enough for all of us—the ones who have suffered and want no one else to experience what they did. None of this comes from a place of malice. It comes from a place of responsibility. This tía was made to feel responsible for many from a young age.

Often, how this tía treats others is a reflection of how she was treated, with some tenderness buried within. They say things like, "La vida es difícil," with little explanation and little comfort to those of us hanging on her every word.

Mi mami is a devout Christian woman, and she believes that her moral superiority is God-ordained. She brandishes warnings and makes judgment calls from a sense of thinking she truly knows what is right and what is wrong. She saw how the rules of her religion could be used against her, and she learned to be ahead of them. To her, everything is in black and white.

She is also the tía who will give you the shirt off her back, and whenever she has any money, she will send it to her mami. She is the glue of her family in a lot more ways than she is given credit for. She tends to carry the burden of being overlooked by making sure no one else is overlooked. She carries the burden of being taken for granted by trying not to take anyone for granted. She will be the one encouraging my dad to reach out to his siblings, to visit them. She forgives too easily. Sometimes to her own detriment. And because she is often left waiting for apologies that never come, she does not allow herself to feel hurt. Her hurt turns into anger, and eventually it turns into judgment—a simple mistake and yet a common one.

> *It is often said that "girls can be much meaner than boys" because they manipulate their social groups in aggressive ways. Few remark that girls are not permitted a physical expression of anger that might allow them to confront the other person with whom they are mad in a different way.*
>
> —Sharon Lamb

The dignified tía was expected to be the mom from a very young age. In her family of origin, she was most likely a co-parent of her siblings. If her siblings were being bullied, it was not the oldest brother who was informed. It was my mami who would roll up her sleeves because as harsh as she can be, she believes in her soul that no one should mistreat her family, and she will use her fists to protect that claim. She fights for others in ways she did not fight for herself, in ways others did not fight for her. As a child, this tía understood that violence must be used if violence is the only method left. This translates often to her words, now as an adult. She can be cruel and quick to cut you down. She has had to learn to be quick—quicker than others who sought to harm her. She had learned to be cruel. She had learned how to survive.

I remember the first time I cut my little sister's bangs. She wanted bangs because I had recently cut my own. I was cutting her hair while it was dry, so as soon as I released her newly cut bangs from my fingers, they bounced up in both directions. This was no big deal. Nothing a good sprinkle of water and a hair iron couldn't fix. But our mami, our dignified mami, saw it and called my sister fea. It was eerie. Her response felt like it did not match the situation or the levity of it all.

That is the thing about being raised by a dignified woman: her inner demons sometimes come out without warning, and as a child I was often left to decipher what it all meant while always assuming I deserved it. Today, I wonder who spoke to her like that.

A dignified tía was often told "no" when she wanted something. She was told "you could never" when she aspired to do something new. And "¿quién te dijo que podías?" when she failed at something. And she might have even been called "fea" by people who were supposed to love her. So while she has learned all that cruelty was not good, she has not learned to deal with why it happened to her, and so it comes out of her at the most unexpected times.

The thing about this type of mami is that she will also vehemently deny her cruelty. She will say or do a thing, have a trigger response, and you will cry for hours, and self-soothe, and then realize one day that you are the only person who remembers the callousness. She forgets, and she never accepts your memories of her hard-heartedness; it is your responsibility to put that somewhere and forget it—like she did, except she did not, and it comes out of her seemingly against her will. It might come out of you, too, one day.

Admitting that she is capable of nastiness is to admit that she is a bad person—the black-and-white thinking ingrained into her own self-assessment. You cannot be a dignified tía if you are caught making mistakes. Good mothers never make mistakes—that is their thinking. Because her world is black-and-white, she will dig her heels in when challenged. She is stubborn.

If you come too close, she will hiss like a cat. She has no reason to believe that you will be kind to her; practically every experience has taught her that people will take advantage of her. The dignified tía holds her head high and her purse close. Earning this tía's trust is how I heal my own mother wound.

I have learned when I meet a dignified tía I am expected to be "good." They operate within the good girl, good woman codes of ethics. I use the proper usted and sit back, not calling attention to myself, earning my place through good behavior. Patience is your best tool when meeting a dignified tía. She is simply a hurt adult who has learned to be hypervigilant with strangers, to read people and keep others at a distance. Contorting myself for a dignified tía is second nature to me, and it's something I mostly resent.

The mother does not greet a daughter as a member of the
chosen caste: she seeks a double in her. She projects onto
her all the ambiguity of her relationship with her self.

—Simone de Beauvoir

Once you manage to get a dignified tía to open up to you, constant work is required to remain in her good graces. If you do something she disapproves of, she will be upset. Let her react brutally about a decision you have made, an outfit you decided to wear, or something you said. The curse of a dignified woman is that she does not want to be alone, even if it feels like that is what she wants. So, with time, she will come down from her high horse. And when she does, she might never admit her wrongdoing, but she will welcome your tenderness when she is ready, and she will respond in kind. Sometimes what is unsaid is just too vulnerable when her vulnerability has been abused. Sometimes admitting she is wrong means admitting that she is imperfect, and it is hard for this tía to show that side to people.

Everyone around the dignified tía has placed high expectations on her because she was the responsible one, the tough one, and the first to leave her parents' home. She forged paths for the rest of her siblings. For those reasons, she sometimes rebukes too harshly those who do not follow her neatly paved path. A path she paved by hand, tearing off her fingernails and scraping her fingers along the way.

The dignified tía is oftentimes judged by others, and unlike other tías who might let the comments glide off their backs, the dignified tía sits and overthinks all that is said to her. In her attempt to shield others, she comes off as heartless and too opinionated. But the dignified tía is a softy, a teddy bear inside, though few get a chance to see it, including her partner.

The dignified tía means well, but she has not found enough tenderness in others to allow her to be soft. It is a circular problem; she creates the distance by being bossy, too demanding. And then she finds herself feeling alone, close only to her convictions. The dignified tía might be the loneliest of your tías because she is the most guarded. It is all a performance; it is about self-preservation to keep others away, but she does not want to be alone.

My compassion for this tía has grown as I have become older. I used to dislike mi mami; I disliked the constant audition and the feeling of never being good enough. I did not understand how someone could be so sharp around the edges. But then I discovered that the secret to getting past the toughness is tenderness. You would never think that; I spent decades not understanding that the toughness is actually protection for all that sweetness within. It was not until, in a mean moment, my little sister said to me, "You are just like mom," that I understood. I had become her, so I began to treat her, reparent her, in ways I wish I would have been parented.

The best thing you can do to a judgmental dignified tía is bombard her with love and affirmation at every turn. She will not know what to do with you, she will not know how to react, and eventually she will accept you, and she will become your protector. She will protect you even when you are nowhere to be seen; she won't allow a bad thing to be said about you.

This is a double-edged sword. Discovering that kindness is a powerful tool because it means you yourself cannot have a bad day. It means understanding that your needs in that relationship must align with hers or disappear entirely. She requires both hands, a full heart, eyes wide open—all of you. With enough warmth from you, her icy stares and clipped responses will soften into warm embraces and hugs.

It is hard, parenting a parent. It is hard to charm someone who should have been charmed by you the second you were born. It is hard to accept having to earn someone's love, and it leaves a wound. This is how you become just like her. The wound of not knowing whether you can trust anyone comes from your mami's side. All of this must be said.

To the daughters of dignified women, realize you will eventually become her, and it takes a lot of self-awareness to improve those circumstances. Much to my own dismay, I am who my little sister has learned to protect herself from because I have not always known where to put my rage, and it spills onto her. My hackles are always raised, but especially when I meet new people. I read as hardened and signal "don't fuck with me" to those who encounter me. These reactions are battle scars, and for a long time I thought this was just my personality type. Some of us have lived too many sad and maddening experiences to look and feel soft and tender, but that does not mean we cannot nurture our tender parts. There is healing to be had, and there are lots of salves to soothe those edges. But learning that someone hurting us does not mean that we are weak has become my own mantra. Learning not to see the world through a black-and-white lens has become instrumental. Learning that my people are fellow dignified tías and even las primas perfectas means that we are the only ones who can stand one another's edges and get to the soft middle. We are also the only ones we trust to call us out. So, spoken like a product of generational trauma, I know that I can be harsh, and I have worked hard to soften my initial responses and expressions, and then I realized that I cannot always do that. I have learned to taste my own blood as I tore through my prickly outer edge to find my tenderness, and now that I have found it within me, I won't stand for her hiding any longer. I am learning to nurture myself. I tell myself I am worthy of softness, even when I am not given it. I tell myself I am worthy of love, even when I am faced with someone who wants me to earn it. I gently run my fingers across my skin and remind myself that touch can be gentle. I am learning to show up tenderly even when I feel afraid, and I hope that I will eventually not be afraid.

To the dignified tía, no matter how much this world has taught you otherwise, you were deserving of grace as a little girl, and you are deserving of love today as an adult. Ultimately, your moral superiority stems from a sense of powerlessness; all these systems have robbed you of your agency and your sense of autonomy. To cling to the one thing that you could was survival, and I applaud your perceptiveness. You were never supposed to feel dignity and pride; they did not want that for you, and yet you found it and raised your head higher than anyone mercilessly trying to control you, be it a man, the government, your church, your employer, or even your own family.

Your dignified stance has earned you social capital within your cultural spaces and family. I do not want to rob you of that, but I want to encourage you to see how you have used similar strategies that were used against you to harm those who have not fully wrapped their minds around the systems that oppress them too. I want to implore you to find the grace that you were not given and give it to yourself. In finding how to be tender to yourself, your own tenderness will flourish for others, and I truly believe that. This world is not going to get nicer, but not allowing it to strip us of our delight is a battle worth fighting. Otherwise, we will continue to raise girls just like us, the good and especially the bad. We know how cruel we can be to ourselves and how that pours over to loved ones more than we would like to admit.

Someone has to end those cycles.

TÍA WHO LOVES PLANTS AND ANIMALS

Feminists point to another kind of damage which is done by separating the mind and body—that is, damage to women. Several feminist writers argue that the oppression of women is linked to the identification of women with bodily natures.

—Naomi R. Goldenberg

I HAVE THIS TÍA WHO CAN BE A BIT PARTICULAR. SHE FEELS LIKE SOMEONE who is perfectly content with being alone, without saying it, and yet she does not look lonely. This tía often retreats to her most trusted fellows. I have this tía who loves all animals and plants.

I am not just talking about owning a dog or liking her one cat a lot. This tía is on another level. This tía feeds strays. Animals know that at a certain time, usually after work, she will show up, and they will get in line waiting for her to deposit the food she puts outside for them. You know exactly who this person is because animals respond to her in ways they rarely respond to others. She also walks around the neighborhood, feeding any outdoor pets she has grown to love. She names her outdoor friends; she loves them, and they rely on her and seem to really come to depend on her. She keeps them alive, and they know it. She becomes their lifeline.

This tía exists in most families, even when it takes a bit for her to appear. In my friend's family, the appearance of this tía came through the younger generation, with sprinkles of this in the grandmother and her green thumb, although her grandmother was not a pet owner. This tía sits with her plants and takes the time to feed them. My tía who loves plants would finish a banana, and at some point she'd find the time to go and cut the peel into pieces and take it outside to her aloe plant. She would place the peels in the dirt around the plant. Her aloe grows twice the size of any aloe plant I have ever seen. As she squats, you can see her lips moving; she is speaking to her plant. If your curiosity makes you walk toward her, she will break her conversation and tell you facts about her plant, even speaking about her plant in third person. She names all her plants and gently caresses her babies. This tía is an angel to these creatures, all living creatures. She is gentle, and that gentleness comes from her relationship to plants and animals. Or maybe her gentleness comes from a profound place of care, which feels heartfelt. To not view humanity as the pinnacle of evolution but as another creature tasked to take care of the planet we all live in is to view the world and its creatures differently.

She does not seek to dominate this earth and the places she inhabits; she seeks to coexist. You do not realize that domination is normalized in your life until you meet her; her contrast feels especially unmasculine. Spaces she occupies are not hers; they feel like they are for everyone, like an invitation.

I was just visiting this tía. I was passing through her town and sent a last-minute text letting her know I was nearby. I honestly did not think she would reply, but of course she did. That is the kind of person this tía is—she is always ready to pour some of herself out to others. As I drove up to her house, a new house she had just purchased, she ran outside to hug me. She greeted me with a huge smile and carried my bags for me. She insisted I stay with her overnight. Then I walked into her home.

Inside, I felt like I was in the Amazon. The sounds of her birds accompanied by the very many houseplants made her living room feel more like one of the last scenes of the living room in *Jumanji* with Robin Williams. It was unreal, and yet it felt so natural to see her in this environment. She seemed so happy here. Her home, in the dead of winter, was warm and lush and full of life. It was a dramatic contrast from the outside.

Several dogs came to greet me, and by several, I mean four. I spotted some kitties watching me intently from afar. As the door stood wide open, not one single animal made their way to the outdoors. They were perfectly happy to be inside and with her.

One wall, the largest wall in her home, was full of cages covered in towels. They were stacked on top of one another, and some cages even went higher than my head. Then she started to remove the towels slowly. I saw about twenty-four birds who started to sing to her as they awoke. Big birds, little birds, loud birds, cuddly birds, birds who spoke, birds who yapped, birds who cooed—it was extraordinary. One bird began reciting the Lord's Prayer, which I remarked upon, and she laughed and said she purchased her from a lady who was clearly Catholic. We both laughed. These birds were magnificent.

As we had dinner later that evening, lasagna, I looked around her kitchen and realized there were more animals than I had initially taken in when I first arrived. She had several tanks with large and small fish inside. She said she had a turtle that was free-range around the home, though I did not see it since it was probably out of sight staying warm. I feel like at some point I lost track of how many animals I saw.

It was hard to keep my eyes in one place without noticing a new animal perched somewhere else. I was in awe at the abundance of animals I saw before me. Animals I thought were destined to be enemies seemed to all reside in this home harmoniously. And as the night went on, as we caught up and shared our intimate memories together and other lived experiences we had while apart, animals would come and sit on her lap, ask for pets, or speak to her from their cages. One bird even insulted us while we had dinner, which added some spice to our meal. It was just two of us, but we were surrounded by life.

It is men's refusal to see themselves as bodies that has rendered the equation of women with body confining and oppressive. In fact, their greater awareness of physical and social contingency gives many women a depth and wisdom that men often lack.

—Naomi R. Goldenberg

This tía is always asking animals for permission to pet them and even to get close to them; animals welcome her into the fold where others are not permitted. When entering a home with a pet, she greets the pets first, letting them know she is there and letting them sniff her and get acquainted with her. When animals have bitten her, she takes that as a sign of her failing to provide that animal with sufficient cues that she meant no harm. She seeks to learn to be more delicate and more aware of animals' cues.

One thing I have learned, as someone who now has an indoor pet, is that how you enter someone's home means everything. Learning to enter someone's home with respect for those who inhabit it is how you earn my dog's respect. My dog seldom barks and seeks to be cuddled by anyone who enters our home, but if you walk in like a colonizer, she will send you a warning bark. In my experience, men tend to have that energy and are more prone to enter homes with more entitlement than other people. This tía has been attuned to that energy for years. She enters a home with pets as she would enter any home of a protective host, with yielding gratitude for the opportunity to share the space. It takes a special type of person to yield to animals because it means you do not view them as conquests.

You will not be surprised to see this tía start a GoFundMe campaign to help pay for the medical bills of a stray cat she takes care of who has come to her beat-up and bleeding. She knows they live outside, and she knows that turf fights are sometimes common practice, but she is connected to these animals. She feels a responsibility to them.

She speaks to her animals like they can speak back, like they are cognizant of what she is saying, like she has a bond with them and we are just lucky enough to witness it. My tía even says, with a smirk, "Me entienden." And it is all fun and games until she says no to her favorite parrot, and the parrot flies off showing visible distaste for the negative response. Their conversations seem less one-sided when these things happen.

This tía finds joy in naming animals, strays and her own. She gives these animals names you would associate with humans, and it is because she sees the humanity of animals. She finds the kindness she needs for herself through being kind to animals. She enjoys finding out her pets' personalities. And when she feels she knows them, she finds a lot of happiness in explaining to a curious onlooker who is who, who does not get along with whom, who is dating, and who acts like siblings. She knows them!

She cannot imagine why anyone would be cruel to animals. Even when she is spiraling and being merciless to herself, she will always find benevolence to pour into these animals she loves. They are a vessel, a manifestation, of her transferred tenderness.

I think it is animals' loyalty that she finds gratifying. When people can be malicious, she finds comfort in the undying loyalty of animals. It overwhelms her to the point that she can cry, watching the unwavering bond between pet and pet parent. Show her an animal being rescued from the grips of starvation and neglect, and you will see her melt into a puddle. She googles who is a reputable rescue organization and who is not. She notices little things no one else does, like simple mannerisms in animals that tell her whether they are taken care of properly. Her observation skills are sharp. She is quick to say, "I do not like that they clipped their dog's ears" or "Adopt, don't buy!" She is always watching how someone reacts to animals because she says that tells her what type of person they are.

My animal-loving tía is not married, but your animal-loving tía might be in a relationship or marriage. In the end, I think the commonalities remain: they are abundantly soft with animals because they see a connection between us and animals in general. She is loved and loves daily. She does not lack companionship; she has it in abundance, actually.

Through this tía, I have learned that animals can become family and trusted life companions, and they can even provide healing through their unwavering devotion. Through this tía I have learned that animals have souls and that they have personalities of their own that develop through their different ages. Through this tía I began to reframe my relationship to the animal kin-dom. To her, I have seen ways in which animals are our furry, feathery, scaly kin. And I see how she is able to do that and be so warm toward them. Being kind to those who cannot advocate and cannot speak up against us feels redemptive, in more ways than anyone can name.

*It has even been suggested that the equation of women
with "mother" nature reveals that the misuse of the environment and the oppression of women have much in
common.*

—Naomi R. Goldenberg

She is attempting to recreate the outdoors inside her
home, and she has found a wonderful way of surrounding
herself with life. Usually, if she is unable to own animals due
to her schedule, limitations in her apartment lease, or simply
knowing that the responsibility may be too much, the plant-
and animal-loving tía can also be an exclusively plant-loving
tía. As with animals, she talks to her plants like they have something to say. To her, plants and animals are related; they need
our help to thrive in environments outside of their original
habitats.

To this tía's family, I hope that you are inspired by her
willingness to see animals and plants as so much more than
items to possess and control. I hope that through her you can
see past her intimate relationship with these living entities
and see the impact our choices have on this planet. I hope that
you can get angry when you hear about a huge corporation
dumping thousands of pounds of clothing waste and creating
an ecological crisis. I hope that when you hear your favorite
frog as a child is now extinct, it makes you push for change.
Individual relationships with creatures and plants will not save
us, but larger conversations and overt change at a corporate
level will.

To this tía, I find your awareness of your spaces very enchanting. I want to know where you found the ability to conjure so much compassion for things that society tells us are less important. To the tía who loves animals, thank you for teaching me an important skill of self-preservation. Through her, I have learned to expand myself beyond a preoccupation with other human beings, and I have taken into account the vastness of this world and the damage we are doing to it. Through her, I have learned to look around me and notice the lack or abundance of areas for wild animals to roam, and to assess what that tells me about said city, neighborhood, mayor, and the like.

I hope that as you are willing to see flaws in your actions that may have led to an animal biting you, this tells you something about human trauma. I think humans can be cruel, but much like animals, it is often traumatic experiences, and people not understanding the hurt that many of us walk with, that make for this cruelty we write off as a human-specific response. Do not write all humans off; sometimes dogs give warning barks much like a hurt human will scream an insult. There are more similarities there than you think.

10

TU TÍA ESCANDALOSA

My thoughts turned toward examining my unac-
knowledged biases toward the Latina women my
mother trained me not to emulate.

—Jillian Hernandez

Tᴜ ᴛíᴀ ᴇsᴄᴀɴᴅᴀʟᴏsᴀ ɪs ᴛʜᴇ ᴀɴᴛɪᴛʜᴇsɪs ᴏғ ʏᴏᴜʀ ᴅɪɢɴɪғɪᴇᴅ ᴛíᴀ ᴀɴᴅ
provides a balance while maintaining the status quo. Tu tía
escandalosa is my most memorable tía. As a daughter of a dignified tía, I was compelled by her unpredictability and she
was a perfect contrast with the dignified tía. While I always
knew what the dignified tía was thinking, I could never predict what the tía escandalosa was thinking. She was a walking
surprise—a sensational one.

Let me tell you about my tía escandalosa. Because she
might be the most unforgettable, she is also the one who gets
narrowed down to just being scandalous. She married into a
family of mostly brothers, who all married dignified women,
women of "good virtue," women their mothers approved of

even if she did not want to approve of them. They married someone "good on paper"; they married someone closer to la prima perfecta. And they are women who pride themselves on being this way. They prided themselves on not caring if they were liked because they were so good that they knew better than to care about what anyone thought. At their core, they had learned how to perform like a good woman, a woman worth marrying, a good mother, a good sister—good, good, good, good. And in their middle-aged years they were set and did not need anyone to approve of them because they knew they were the epitome of what was asked of them for their gender.

My tía escandalosa was not only significantly younger, but she wore tight clothes and red lipstick; she drank, cursed, and spoke to men like she was their equal. She had male friends, and she had a certain level of comfort around men. Because she moved differently than the dignified women in my family, she was judged.

I come from women who aspire to become saints. Women who do anything that dares to defy that heavy burden must be cast off. To challenge our devotion to the thing that might end us, to show defiance to the things that now define us, is to ridicule our duty as women. And to them, "rules" must be followed.

Judgment is the tool of the dignified señoras. Judgment spurred by indignation is their weapon of choice. And it is heavy to sit on the receiving end of said judgment. The training from womanhood to sainthood is arduous and lengthy because it teaches us to quelch the spirit within ourselves. The spirit of rambunctiousness that is evident in the tía escandalosa is inescapable.

Keeping that spirit alive, or allowing her to do so, is a threat to the status quo. If one of us breaks from the mold and faces no consequences, then what is the point of the mold? To keep the order of business, the women in my family have become experts at snuffing out any spirit other than the one and only Espíritu Santo. This sense of duty to correct improper womanhood comes at you from a young age, and though there is more room to fight against it, girls are often facing bullying if they do stand out, if they are tomboys, if they do not care about boys when they are perceived to be old enough to care, and if they do not fixate on feminine performance. There is this sense of correction that happens within our own circles that just continues to grow as we grow. When you are younger it is easier to ignore all that, but as you grow older you find it harder to laugh off their corrections and their prodding about why you are doing something "weird" and why you insist on doing that thing they do not approve of.

Bullying exemplifies a contextually available feminine resource which enables girls to simultaneously subordinate gender nonconforming girls and normalize certain gendered practices. Gender deviant girls are often the targets of and thus victimized by verbal and physical abuse and social isolation.

—Justin Charlebois

Mi tía escandalosa loves to dance. When the booze is flowing and the music gets turned on late into the night, this tía will be the first to start dancing, while all the other relatives wait for the liquid courage to hit. I remember my tía escandalosa firstly by her laugh. When she laughed, she laughed with her entire body, throwing her curly head of hair back, showing every tooth in her mouth all the way up to her molars. She was a sight to see. She was a spectacle in her singularity among the women in my family, especially among my older tías who thought she was too loud. I was kept from her because the women in my family know how to raise other dignified señoras-in-the-making. The training is early, and it is constant. And the messaging around this tía was clear: do not be like her.

Your tía escandalosa can dance every genre of Latin music, and she has the hips to do it well. She's the first to start dancing and the last to leave the party. For Noche Buena, this tía prepares like she is training for a marathon. She paces herself and announces that fact to everyone. She wants everyone to know that she is ramping up to have a good time, and she wants to have that good time with others.

Every sala party turns into a club when this tía is around, and she knows it. In the heat of a great song, she will raise her hands in the air and clap, dropping her head back with her eyes closed, stomping her feet to the beat of the music, and flat out losing herself in the moment. She can feel the music, and her body responds to it. She is lost in the moment and enjoys it to the fullest extent.

She is the life of the party, the center of gossip, and the purveyor of even more gossip. And I do not mean this pejoratively—gossip can be a useful tool practiced by these types of tías to heed warnings, teach lessons, and share crucial information. Her gossip can be wonderful and fun, but the gossip about her has the power to become unethical. This kind of gossip can be used to clip someone's wings even when all they are doing is soaring above our heads. In envidia, or unprocessed self-hatred and anger, we can become expert wing-clippers.

It was always easy to see this tía as someone who felt aspirational, though I knew better than to say that out loud. I knew better than to defy mi mami, who spent a lot of energy indoctrinating me into being the type of good woman she saw herself as embodying. The type of woman she knew to be rewarded by society at large; the type of woman a man would pick as his wife. Even when I clearly saw my tía escandalosa get picked by my uncle, it somehow felt like it was temporary. She was not treated like a permanent and reliable family member who could be trusted to have a significant place in our family as a whole. She was seen as trouble, and the point was not to be perceived in that way.

Whereas men are rewarded for exhibiting self-confidence through terms such as assertive, go-getter, and stud, women are viewed as overstepping the boundaries of conventional femininity and accordingly face disparaging epithets such as aggressive, bitch, or slut.

—Justin Charlebois

This tía is younger, and in the age gap, the tías in my family found someone to gang up on. All the other children of this family, the children of the brothers and their wives, were around the same age, and every brother had managed to have two girls and a boy. We were bonded and thick as thieves. This tía was younger, and she and my tío did not have kids while the cousins were all children. When our parents all hung out, the kids always played together till the adults grew tired of one another. I have so many memories of these weekend gatherings. That sense of family felt so special. She felt integral to those dynamics, even when she was clearly treated differently. It was not until she had a few kids that she was treated better. Not well, just better than before.

The thing about tu tía escandalosa is that she is not here to be palatable, and her husband seems to not only understand that but love that aspect about her. Her husband is actually your favorite tío, often, because he does not find satisfaction in muting others around him for his ego. He has this silent confidence that puts everyone at ease, and you can't dislike a tía who clearly has the attention of your favorite tío. He's your dad's favorite brother, and he is the most handsome tío too. I think gentle men, men who are gentle, just feel more attractive when you are accustomed to men who approach girls and women as assessments. Pass or fail. Marriage material or whore. Good or bad.

But I remember this tía; I remember her wit and her outfits. I remember how mi tío looked at her adoringly; he loved her. He was crazy about her. Seeing that type of love, young love, it was bewitching. They are who I picture in my head when I picture my idealized childhood. They were two good-looking young people; my uncle had a mullet and wore bleach-washed jeans with button-down shirts tucked into his pants. Mi tía wore miniskirts of all different colors, but my favorite was her purple miniskirt she wore with a matching top. They looked like movie stars.

This tía can be too much for some, and she has heard this her entire life. She has been told to simmer down, to be quiet, or to mute herself more than any other woman in your life—and that is because she threatens others by existing differently and still getting the thing they all were told to strive for: a man. This tía and tu tía la loca may sound similar, but there is one distinct difference, and that difference is that the tía escandalosa has a place in family gatherings, whereas the la loca has no place. And what I mean by that is that your tía escandalosa is married; she does the thing she is supposed to do, but she does it while bending the rules. La tía loca breaks the rules entirely. The tía escandalosa is vulnerable to snickering and judgment as attempts to tame her. But she can still exist in family circles because even as they've ranked her as inferior to them, they cannot banish her even when they want to do just that. The loca cannot do much of that because tu tía loca does not see value in male companionship. Keeping her around is accepting her truth, and no one wants to publicly claim such a thing.

Tu tía escandalosa, on the other hand, feels like a trickster, like she's too good to be true. To be a woman and exist unabashedly and get a good man—that does not happen, that should not happen, so she must be bad. Deep inside her, she must be a bad woman to prove everything that has been taught to these women. They make her the scandal to prove that their choices are correct. She shows all the internalized sexism in female circles an alternative that may not always work out, but sometimes it does, and when it does, it feels forbidden. In its forbiddenness we grow envious, and ultimately, we grow distrusting of this person. Living in the forbiddenness means that there is a price to pay; we all pay a price.

> *Black and Latina women and girls who embody aesthetics of excess are "thought to be morally wanting by both dominant society and other indigenous group members."*
> —Cathy J. Cohen

I have this tía who is married to the youngest of seven brothers on my dad's side of the family. Marrying the youngest boy put her in a deficit, especially when entering a family of dignified señoras who had to contend with a dignified mother-in-law. In a society that expects women to be virtuous and flat, to be anything but that means that you will be viewed with disdain. Her plight might be lonesome in her family, but she is not alone. She is not the only escandalosa out there. And in some families, they might all be escandalosas together, and the dignified tía might be the outcast. Yet society will reward the dignified tía in the same ways that the escandalosa will be shunned.

It would take me years to fully appreciate this tía because as much as the other women in my family love her, they also criticize her the most. So much so that you begin to think maybe she is as bad as they say, but your eyes tell you a different story. You are told you don't know anything if you try to defend her. But maybe her biggest crime is that she does not rein herself in. As I write all this down, I can already see my own mami rolling her eyes at my "generosity," as she will call it. I have grown accustomed to being told I do not know anything about the real world whenever I have dared to glorify any aspect of the tía escandalosa.

Age has shown me that this tía is to be protected and encouraged. A tía this glorious cannot be tamed, nor should she be. That's true even when everything around her, including most of the information you have heard about her, seems to want to paint her in the worst light. One particular rumor I have heard said and repeated is that my cousins, the children of this tía, are not related to me. Whenever I have asked why they think that, why this is being said about this tía, I am told that it is obvious based on their lack of similarities with my uncle and one another. No facts, just speculations. The tía escandalosa married into the family, and she seems to be too friendly. And your tío seems unperturbed by these rumors that have surely made it to his ears. I do not come from coy people.

For generations women accepted the role of legitimizing humans through marriage to a man. They agreed that a human was not acceptable unless a man said so. Without that "masculine" protection, the mother is vulnerable.
—Clarissa Pinkola Estés

This tía must've also heard these rumors, but she still greets us all with warm hugs and no sign of resentment. Any attempts to vilify her, we have learned, have only reflected poorly on those doing that type of gossip. But those of us observing and trying to figure out what is really happening know that it is actually the ones spreading unsubstantiated gossip like the rumors about your cousins who deserve the scorn. In attempting to forcefully domesticate her through bullying, what they have managed to do is create enemies among those of us who are watching from the sidelines while forming our own opinions.

To the family of the tía escandalosa, I hope you take the time to think about why you feel the need to shame other women for doing the things you might secretly want to do. I understand feeling anger toward your own indoctrination, but then get some vindication on those who tamed you by freeing yourself. You will find more joy in that than in taming someone else. You might even feel more alive, and if you lose people in doing all that, may that be a loss of theirs and not the other way around.

I have seen it, and I often find myself catching this instinct to suppress someone's spirit because of a hurt within myself. That is how generational trauma is passed down. One small, seemingly insignificant critique can turn someone away from something they love due to shame. Shaming someone is powerful, and it can change someone entirely.

This tía seems to live the fullest life, partying with her own friends and taking trips with her husband. Her family is a priority, but her exhilaration is also a priority. To this tía escandalosa, thank you for not smothering the fire within you. It is your fire that has kept many warm during nights when the indoctrination felt suffocating to us, even if we could not even name that. Seeing you stay, even when others want to extinguish you, shows us to stay when we want to even if we're up against great odds. I also want to encourage you to consider not shouldering their snickers like you do not hear them; it would do dignified women some good to face consequences to their public shaming. You might have an ally in the tía loca—find her and befriend her, if you have not already. She is out there, exiled, and maybe the two of you can build something together. Maybe the two of you can provide safe spaces for the various rejects in our families. Maybe the two of you can create some wonderful trouble, just as they predicted, but not like they ever imagined.

To mi tía escandalosa, thank you for teaching me que cuando llega el viernes, el cuerpo lo sabe! When I find myself dancing the night away with my own nieces, nephews, and niblings, I think of you fondly. I channel you whenever I am scared because I know that you would have chosen the unknown over the safe choice any day.

11

PRIMA WHO DOESN'T LIKE OTHER WOMEN

*What is especially insidious and psychologically destruc-
tive about sexism is its closeness. We do not have distance
from it. It is in our homes and in our own families from
the earliest years, and it comes under such baffling and
seductive disguises as nurturance and romantic love.*

—Bonnie Burstow

WE ALL KNOW THIS PRIMA, AND SOME OF US MAY HAVE BEEN THIS PRIMA
at some stage in our lives. The prima who does not like female
company, or purports not to. The prima who when all the
women gather in the kitchen and dining room, she stays with
the men in the living room. I know this prima because I have
been her. The "guys' girl," who wears that title with pride. I
had no significant friendships with women other than my
cousins till my late twenties. In some ways I avoided them, and
in other ways they were discouraged.

My prima who seems to hate the company of women is sweet, but she gravitates toward the primos and tíos more. I envy the perceived ease with which she just seems comfortable around these men. But I know better; I know that the heartbreak is almost upon her. And yet I want to bottle that hope. The hope that she will be different, the hope that she will be treated better, the hope that she will be the exception and not the rule.

When I was the prima who hated women, in so many ways it was because I loved my dad. I was mi papi's favorite. And in a patriarchal household, when a man picks you, it feels extra special. I felt proud to be a "daddy's girl" until I began to realize how much of our relationship was contingent on my malleability.

As I got older, as I began to exercise my critical thinking skills and ask more questions, the more of an annoyance I seemed to become to my dad. Eventually, the words "sos igualita a tu mami" rolled out of his mouth a little too easily, like they had been sitting there all along waiting to be used against me even when I was good, even when I was doting. The sting of those words was in the undertones because in our closeness, I had become his confidant, and I knew how much he resented mi mami. I also understood that he benefitted from their relationship; it was convenient for him, and having me around to agree with his every conclusion he made about her made my company valuable to his life. But when I became just like her, in his eyes, I was no longer worth much to him. He passed me off. I did not choose to leave the comfort of that bond; I was thrown out of it. Once the words were said, I knew I had been demoted in his eyes.

> *As she [the daughter] gets older, she is more often lumped with the mother (woman) to whom she feels superior. Intermittently she feels furious with father for going along with the unfair status change and in the process may switch affection to others. More fundamentally, however, she blames mother for passing on the curse of womanhood, often while continuing to see father (man) as a possible savior.*
>
> —Bonnie Burstow

All the things I hated about women were the things I was *taught* were despicable about women, through my own papi, brother, and secret boyfriends. These were not my original thoughts; in fact, my thoughts were copy-pasted words I had heard about women from men in my life. Chisme is a good example of that. I was taught that chisme was a despicable thing women did exclusively. Which is untrue, and chisme is crucial to oral traditions. Chisme has a bad reputation because when we think of chisme, we think of women. And our hatred of women transcends women and trickles into things we associate with them. Words like bitch, slut, cunt, and whore are all female-gendered words with no similar male counterparts. We do not get to be chefs; even when we are creating magic in our family kitchens, we are home cooks. We are not fashion designers—even if we are making quinceañera dresses for the community—but costureras. We do not get to be the ones passing on generational knowledge and teaching ancestral lessons; instead, we get called chismosas. All this belittling of female labor is just normalized misogyny.

> *While men's entry into feminized professions actually increases the occupations' social prestige, the feminization of certain occupations is negatively viewed.*
>
> —Justin Charlebois

As I have shed my own need for male approval, I have seen myself move from being the prima who hates other women to the prima (and now tía) who loves women. When my family gathers, the children usually play and go off to either outside in front of the house or in the backyard. Then the men go off to watch television in the living room while the women are expected to provide the food for the gathering, so our usual meeting place is the kitchen and dining room. If your household does not adhere to this division of labor, then bless you, but unfortunately, unless the men are grilling, I have yet to see this totally reversed where women get to sit in the living room the entire time while the men do this type of labor. Unless the gathering is with queer folks, the division of labor in even the most progressive hetero spaces is often gender-based. From the Caribbean to Central America, Miami, and even Nashville, I have found myself in dining rooms and kitchens alongside mostly women while the men enjoy one another's company. Our designated areas become the kitchen and the dining area, in homes where these two rooms are one. If men want to sit with us, they come to these areas, and if we want to be with the men, we will make our way to their designated spots.

The women in my family come alive and become the best versions of themselves when they are together. We become the versions that many of the husbands do not get to see because of internal marital conflicts and overall social-gender inequalities that are still in effect in a lot of marriages. When they get together, it is like the women in my life remember who they are. Because of this, the men usually stay away. All their sins of that week will come up if they attempt to cross into the women's territory. We stand ready to defend one another; we become an army of scorned women who will not be contained in the company of our crew. We will incite a dispute, if poked enough, so the men have learned not to poke.

I love the company of my female relatives, so I end up in the kitchen, picking at food prep. We laugh harder and we talk more in-depth about our lives. It is gossip hour, and I am an active participant in these engagements. The older I have gotten, the more I look forward to these gatherings. In these family gatherings, there are floaters. Not many folks can float, and not many are talented enough to float without becoming a nuisance to either group. Floating is discouraged; only a handful can float, and everyone understands who can and cannot float (*see the tía escandalosa chapter*).

It is easy to spot a woman who does not care for other women. A pick-me. A woman who wants to be chosen by men time and time again. She scorns women the loudest. Some go-to anti-women jabs I expertly utilized were: "Women are

all drama"; "A las mujeres solamente les gusta chismear"; or
the classic "Women are just too emotional." You have probably heard all of these old and tired statements; they are common practice. These statements are a ruse meant to distract
from what is actually happening—the systemic oppression of
women. Women-hating is a default personality type for many
girls, but it must eventually include self-reflection to free ourselves from this self-hating and reductive mentality.

> *Daughter/victim is set up to hate mother/tyrant.…*
> *Woman is associated with the injury and blamed, while*
> *man appears to have nothing whatever to do with it,*
> *benefits, and is absolved.*
>   —Bonnie Burstow

My own desires for winning over and gaining male
approval were most visible in how I rejected the women in my
life. As my body began to change, I started to resent the ways
I was treated differently even when I felt the same. It became
obvious that this shift meant proximity to the lesser of the two
parental figures. My hostility with women was really a reflection of my hostility toward the unequal treatment I was bound
to receive.

The prima who hates other women is usually young, but
not exclusively. The prima who does not like other women says
she does not like the hustle and bustle of female culture, along
with the good and bad that come from engaging with that
many women. I outgrew this anti-women stance, as many of
us do, because at the end of the day, male approval requires

self-denial, but arriving at this realization is neither pretty nor fun. In fact, it is heartbreaking. Accepting our inferior status in society (not my own words, but rather what society shows me/us) and making lemonade out of the position we find ourselves in.

Ultimately, I believe that what the prima who hates women is attempting to do is distance herself from our inevitable destination within oppression. As if we asked for it—as if we often have a choice in the matter. The women in my life openly discuss the things they are dissatisfied with in such matter-of-fact tones, and that can feel painful when you are younger. It can feel like a warning you are not ready to hear. Maybe this prima cannot articulate that she hates how we reflect her future, a potential prison within heterosexual partnerships. Maybe what she really wishes is to free herself, and sooner or later, she will realize that we might be her most potent allies in that fight.

> *She first discovers the hierarchy of the sexes in the family experience; little by little she understands that the father's authority is not the one felt most in daily life, but it is the sovereign one.*
>
> —Simone de Beauvoir

There were elements of parenting that began to get passed off to mi mami, and that is when the distance between mi papi and I began. My mom and I began to build a life of secrecy. It was my mom who taught me how to roll up my bloody sanitary napkins in toilet paper, and then also to clump a few more pieces of toilet paper on top of it, to hide the shame of bleeding regularly. We spoke in whispers to each other, once a month. Eventually, we would hide shopping bags together inside grocery bags or leave them in the car till my dad fell asleep and sneak the bags upstairs. We would giggle, knowing we were outsmarting the *head of our household.* We were attempting to resist that control he had over all our lives as the sole breadwinner. In our secrecy we gained a sense of power back, or so we thought.

We began to build a relationship based on our shared fear of him and our shared distrust of his control over us. His ability to build us up and tear us down felt hostile to me very quickly. This is when I began to run toward other women. And when I ran toward them with tears streaming down my face because it meant that my relationship with mi papi would never be the same, as he had ordained it, I discovered something beautiful. I discovered a tenderness in these women that I needed; I discovered an understanding in their hugs.

To me, the women are the entertainment, fashion, humor, and life lessons. The laughter that booms out of the women-filled rooms I stepped into, it was contagious. While with mi papi I had to be a reflection of his thoughts to be loved, the women who awaited took delight in me. This is what I want the prima who does not like other women to experience. I want her to experience the delight of someone watching you find yourself instead of the delight of becoming a reflection of a man's own thoughts and expectations.

Anyone can see that identification with mother means drudgery and powerlessness. Collusion with father is an obvious pull, and father generally is only too ready to collude. The daughter's live intelligence after is attractive, compared to the dullness of his exhausted wife-turned-drudge; and in the early years this intelligence is not sufficiently threatening that it need be snuffed out. Often father and daughter look down on mother (woman) together. They exchange meaningful glances when she misses the point. They agree that she is not bright as they are, cannot reason as they do.

—Bonnie Burstow

I also think that the men embrace this prima to prove something to themselves. I think they envy our gatherings. I think they resent us for not wanting to be with them even when everything around us has told us otherwise; in these kitchen gatherings, we defy that norm. I think I would resent us if I were in their position. But in their resentment, they do not try to transform their own relationships; rather, they continue to subject the malleable primas who are vulnerable to them.

The commitment to the lie that men could ever possibly be better, smarter, funnier is precisely why we all notice that one young prima who keeps her distance from us women. More poignantly, I know I judge her, and some others may judge her as well. I judge her because I begrudge the part of myself who once thought I could be different. I judge her because I am angry at the parts of me men took advantage of

in my impressionable years. And maybe that is why that prima
stays away—maybe she feels all of that. With men she might
not even have time to feel anything, for a while, if she simply
molds herself to their needs as I once did. There is perceived
safety in the way you can become invisible alongside them.

> *Most women spend countless hours listening to the
> monologues of male friends, hearing their bragging, and
> empathizing with their tales of woe. It takes active and
> ongoing refusal to make a dent in the imbalance. Women
> who refuse to listen or who demand more semblance of
> equality are dismissed as "cold bitches" by the average
> man, as well as by [women who sympathize with men],
> and are often seen as problematic even by those who
> pride themselves on being politically aware.*
>
> —Bonnie Burstow

When you gather that many women who are related, you
get unsolicited advice by the handfuls. It comes with the territory. We come from vast age groups: the tías, the abuela and
her sisters, the primas who also come in different age ranges.
When you have that much experience in one room accompanied by that much love, the unsolicited advice seems to pour
out of us all. The guidance of these women feels pushy because
it is. But they are pushing you to grow and be better. The men
in your life might actually be less pushy, especially if what they
like about you is their own reflection. Our minds already tell
us men are better, so we cannot quite see the error in that for
some time.

Together, when the women in my life gather, nos desahogamos. But when men are teaching you, through glares and eye rolls, that our opinions are inferior, it feels like too much to sit and listen to these mujeres. Unfortunately, while many of us can swim furiously against what feels like an overwhelming current of chatter, from every angle, some of us are just too entrenched in anti-women positions to manage. Those of us who just want to blend, we cannot walk away from those encounters with women who are fighting to feel important in a world that tells them they are not and still feel whole. Instead, those encounters damage us and make us feel inadequate. It's the opposing realities that are at the root of this discomfort. If society tells us men are superior, and our tías tell us who "really" runs the house while serving her husband his plate of food as if he cannot make it himself, then what is the truth? This much dissonance, without the proper tools to understand it all, can be overwhelming. But the truth is that we are all living in the dissonance—some of us just have more years living with it and getting numb to it.

Most women both claim and detest their feminine condition; they experience it in resentment.

—Simone de Beauvoir

The women in my family become judge and jury when we are together, and while the intention is always to help, our deliveries can seem to lack compassion. We are so eager to redeem our existence in the younger generations that we risk scaring them away. For the prima who does not like other women, her disdain for those women-centric gatherings comes from having absorbed misogynistic interpretations. Her only solace is in being around the men who have built and cemented those negative misconceptions of women to silence us. Sometimes when we feel powerless, we lean into oppressing those with less power to gain our footing. It is a gut reaction, and a problematic gut reaction that we must check, but it is prevalent nonetheless.

We are too much when we are together, too much as we overflow out of ourselves. When not together, we cannot exist in the same ways. These moments together, as tías and primas, they really cement our sense of worth. These gatherings are life-giving for most of us while leaving those of us who are less prepared feeling less-than.

To the prima who hangs out with the men, what have you lost in your distance from us? Do you feel respected by the men, or does it all feel conditional? When you inevitably come to us, will you find allies in the primos and tíos you invested so much energy into? I wonder if too much time with the men who benefit from our partnerships while exploiting our powerlessness is how we infect the feminine spaces that are necessary fuel for us. Were we all women-hating women one day, and this is the natural progression? Did we all get left and not choose to leave? Where does that heartbreak get mended, and who mends it?

To the women who rebuke the women-hating prima, do you reflect enough on how you may also hate women, and that is why you insist on fixing yourself through this prima and the rest of us? Do we reflect enough on how much we may hate the state of our existence within our patriarchal marriages? Are our gatherings enough? Is survival enough? I do not have the answers to these questions. I simply must write them down to keep myself from going numb to my own oppression.

To the prima who hangs out with the men, be assured that we are patiently waiting for you to find your way to us. The day will come when someone will break your heart, or a male boss will make you feel lower than gum on a shoe, and you will come to us because we will take your side—judge and jury—knowing that "todos son iguales." Mostly, I hope you know that even with all our flaws and imperfect responses to our ongoing subjugation, we will welcome you with open arms. May we all become one another's teachers because maybe the prima who hated women but realized what was really happening, maybe this prima will become angry enough to start our revolutions. Maybe this prima will carry our anger, our tears, our stories, and scream loudly so that enough primas and tías may hear and change it all for us. May we all show one another more grace as we attempt to make sense of this state of our existence, better than yesterday but with so much work left to be done.

12

THE CHILDLESS TÍA

Socially constructed notions of masculinity and femininity or social actions and behaviors that we attribute to and thus associate with men and women can arguably both empower and disempower individuals.

—Justin Charlebois

WE ALL KNOW THIS TÍA. THE FACT THAT SHE IS CHILDLESS MAY BE THE main characteristic that defines her. Your mami talks about it often. When the women all gather, they lament this at some point or another. Your childless tía's "predicament" teaches you, through them, that being childless is a shame, a problem, an issue. This tía becomes imprinted in your memories as the tía without kids through other adults who insist this is something worth noting. I can tell you how many childless women I met in my childhood because it was spoken about openly: three. That is how many women I knew personally as a child who were childless. They were all of a marriageable age, and so their lack of male partnership was seen as a problem that needed to be fixed.

These women seemed irregular, from where I stood as a child myself. But this tía is not as irregular as you may think; she is in fact more common than she is made out to be. This tía looks no different than all your other tías. She is just as tall, gets her hair cut just as often, and wears her skirt at the same length as the other tías. Standing side by side with all her sisters, nothing about her feels significant. Yet, the way they treat her makes it seem like a glaring difference that cannot be contained within one conversation or moment.

A version of this tía may still live at home. If she is childless because she never married, then it probably means that she was raised traditionally where women have sex only in marriage and children are products only of a loving heterosexual marriage. She may lament that this was her fate, but she is rewarded by her parents and society for doing what was "right" or "best." The moral judgment of becoming a single mother does not weigh on her. What she may openly mourn is the lack of a husband, life passing her by, "si tan solo…"

She may be married but experiencing infertility. This is something you have probably seen your family pray about at length, and if she is older, they prayed till they ran out of prayers, and then one day they just stopped. They stopped talking about it. They stopped pushing the topic, but the emptiness of something missing and longed-for remains in the air. That is what compulsory motherhood means. Womanhood becomes directly equated to motherhood, and a deficit in that department must mean failure, and we signal that to her even when we think we are not doing so.

In a culture that overvalues heterosexual families, women are raised to live up to normative culture, and that also means child production by default. Women are still expected to have children; there is no question about that. Just ask a recently married woman of childbearing age how often she has been asked when she will start having children.

What happens when you find out something that was assumed about you, like fertility, turns out to be untrue? You become a problem everyone wants to help solve. Your family may push this tía to look into other options, like adoption. They may flippantly suggest it. But as a childless tía myself, I think there is a special place in hell for someone who suggests adoption upon learning about your infertility. The assumption that the childless tía who wants children has not searched high and low to find answers to her socially imposed "purpose" of becoming a mami is offensive. And casually offering a solution that you came up with in the thirty seconds it took you to process her infertility is just lazy at best and outright insulting at worst. It is disrespectful to think that your childless tía who wants children has not thought about it all. It is ludicrous to think you can possibly have a new alternative solution to her "problem." And it is just rude to think someone is asking you, a non-medical provider, to offer solutions for something you do not even fully understand.

Another version of your childless tía, and a place the tía who is infertile may eventually find herself in, is the one of not wanting children. There is a version of this tía occurring more and more every day as women become more educated and access to birth control continues to be the norm. Obviously, this is something happening in more elite and wealthier communities, but there is a growing brigade of women who have no desire to have children. Some may have never desired them.

Even a generous mother who sincerely wants the best for her child will, as a rule, think it wiser to make a "true woman" of her, as that is the way she will be best accepted by society.

—Simone de Beauvoir

When I first got my period, I was celebrated for my ability to have children. My mom spoke to me and said, "Ahora ya eres una mujer," simply because my uterus lining had begun to shed. My womanhood was immediately connected to my uterus because of what my uterus signaled to everyone. My womanhood was inextricably linked to my potential motherhood. As if anyone with a uterus can reproduce; it was a sign of becoming a woman, and in my context that meant that I could become a mother. To say that had no impact on me would be a lie, and to say that it was not a disappointment when I discovered I cannot have babies without medical assistance would also be a lie. I felt like my life had no purpose, in fact. And I had to contend with years of socializing after the fact. To cis mothers rearing girls, their daughters becoming eventual mothers feels natural because to them it might have been natural.

We are often raising girls to become mothers, above all else. As a little girl, your toys are babies, baby dolls. When we think of "boy" toys we think of guns, cars, trucks, balls. And what we think of as "girl" toys are usually mini kitchens, dolls to take care of, Barbies to mimic home life, and just projections of becoming a caretaker.

My education at home was a childrearing one. When my little sister was born, I was tasked with looking out for her even when I was not the oldest child, just the oldest daughter. My gender meant I was automatically viewed as more nurturing even though we know those things are not correlated. I was regularly told to prepare for motherhood and for caretaking.

There is no such thing as maternal "instinct."
—Simone de Beauvoir

The tía who has chosen to not have kids and the tía who cannot have kids have the same destinations but different stories. They are both navigating the same questions regularly. I think true freedom comes when they become desvergüenzas about it.

"Desvergüenza" is one of my favorite words in Spanish. The literal translation of the word means someone who is without shame, shameless. What happens when you are a childless woman, in a society that still very much prefers mothers over women, is that they get prescribed a sense of shame. People feel shame for the childless tía like they were presumably born with all the "right" parts to become a mom, and they went ahead and wasted it. People feel shame for the childless tía; people will say they feel sad for her, even if the childless tía shows no sadness for herself. The childless tía is tasked with feeling that shame, mirroring that shame, in order to proceed. But not too much. Don't make fertile women feel bad for having healthy reproductive organs. The childless tía has to feel the *right* amount of shame. Like they missed out on their "greatest purpose," but they are lucky to still be alive. The childless tía is tasked with walking a delicate line, which quite frankly is impossible. It is an impossible task added to the impossible reality that the childless tía dared to live outside of her predefined gender-specific purpose.

So what if the childless tía ventures into feeling no shame? What if the childless tía in a family is happily childless and maybe even successful and thriving because all her money and all her energy is put into herself? And then, what if the childless tía becomes desvergüenza about it?

I'll tell you what happens to me when I tell people with children that I do not have any with a smile on my face. Those people scramble to find my shame. Their questions that follow reflect an attempt to place that shame on me. They ask if I want them (children), to which I have learned "yes" means they can put the shame on that word. Like "Aha! She *is* unhappy. Surely I would be too if I had not become a parent." "Aha! I did the right thing." "Aha! That makes sense to me." So I say, "No."

And in my "no," they scramble again and ask if I have always not wanted them, again trying to find a repository for the shame, and again I lie and say "no" in an effort to not give any room for this shame. Even if I am lying, in refusing to tell the truth, I am refusing them the opportunity to find a place for a shame I do not want, a shame I do not feel.

And then the conversation usually ends. They change the subject. They lose interest. My closest friends do not have kids, have only one child, or they are single mothers. People who understand that parenting is not something you can autopilot understand that not everyone should be parents. Those people also seem to understand that not everyone wants to become a parent. In normative society, I am tasked with carrying shame for my childlessness, and maybe not so coincidently, I have ended up with chosen family who will not allow that shame to take root within me.

I have found that once people know I do not have children, new potential friendships dissolve. I am often met with odd attempts at connection from parents through Hallmark card statements like, "I bet you would have been a wonderful mom!" "One day when you are not thinking about it, it'll happen." Or my personal favorite: "Well, you can have my kids!" followed by forced laughter on their end. Childless women are tasked with comforting parents who may be starting to realize that they might be in over their heads. That maybe they did not understand the bigness of their task as parents. Childless women are tasked with managing a lot of unspoken rules, and that is the true shame here.

Growing up, I barely saw my parents interact with childless women unless we were related to them in one way or another. A childless tía is never a matriarch because she has no disciples. Nobody wants to follow the childless tía's footsteps or teach their children that the existence of the childless tía is necessary and maybe should be celebrated.

I did not decide that I was not going to have kids. Instead, money and time became my worst opponents. At first, my body told me it wasn't going to create a life "naturally" through multiple miscarriages. I never got answers to so many questions because pursuing answers takes resources; it takes money. And the next thing I knew, I was getting divorced. After that period in my life, I committed myself to dating. I married too young, and I found myself wanting to explore, sexually and otherwise.

My abortions were choices I made because I was not sure what my body would do with another pregnancy, and waiting for a miscarriage is not my idea of a good time. I got two abortions out of a sense of control. Divorce made me feel out of control. Becoming a single woman and turning thirty made me feel out of control, and I was not sure I wanted to be a single mother; I did not have the means to make that call. States create single mothers and then give them abysmal choices for medical care and schools, not to mention a gendered pay gap that makes it impossible to make a living wage. My abortions gave me options to live a life not paved for me, but rather a life I could pave for myself. I did not decide that I was never going to have kids. That didn't feel like the decision I made.

By 2019, I had a budding career as a writer. At thirty-five years old, I signed my first book deal with a major publisher and started writing my first book.

Covid-19 hit, and the world got scary. Within weeks the country shut down, a bomb went off in downtown Nashville, and a tornado wreaked havoc in the surrounding areas of our city. I got scared of what a future would be like in a time that felt apocalyptic. I am still scared about what a future will look like on a dying planet.

And now I'm almost forty, and I guess I'm not having children.

It wasn't that I decided not to have kids. It was more like I decided not to pressure myself into doing something that I was unable to do given the timing of everything.

Somewhere along the way, I got to focus on myself and found it intoxicating. At thirty-eight years old, I have money for the first time in my life. I have money to pay my bills and buy art and explore my interests. I am healing parts of myself that financial insecurity in my childhood stunted. I found healing because I was able to experience safety for the first time. I began therapy and found monsters in my closet. Monsters that haunted me, day in and day out. And I have gotten to make friends with my monsters; I have taken the power they had over me.

I have found joy outside of motherhood. A joy I didn't know was possible because I didn't know women who were happy and childless. I knew childless women who openly spoke about their misfortune of not becoming mothers. But I found joy in the experience of not becoming a mom. A joy that feels all mine and all-encompassing.

I have found that I have expensive taste. I have found a sense of freedom that I never even knew I could have. And all of this came from having time to focus on myself, selfishly and wholeheartedly.

That is not to say that I don't feel sadness or grief over not having become a mother. It's not that black-and-white; few things are. I have cried before when I think of what I could have been. I have spent the majority of my life thinking I would be a mother someday. My parents, life, and society have ingrained in me a desire, and it is hard to differentiate myself from that strategically planted *want*. I wonder what my kid would have been like. I dream about the life I could have given them.

But what if the trade for motherhood is that I never got to fully meet myself? Would I make that trade? The answer is no. The answer is clear to me, unless a child appears in my life out of the blue. The path has been taken, and I'm on it. I'm a childless woman—a never mother and so much more than that.

Can you imagine having an adult in your life who showed you what life could be like if given the option and not force-fed motherhood? Can you imagine how full life could feel even without children? Can you imagine teaching your children that fulfillment comes in all types of ways?

Your childless tía is just like all your other tías, but at some point, she made a decision to either eternally grieve a motherhood she will not have or become okay with who she is and what her happiness could mean to those around her. Your childless tía, the one who is childless by choice, may not come around much, and it could be because she is busy living a different life, a wonderfully full life despite what anyone might tell you about her.

To the family of the childless tía, the gift that comes from being a childless woman is an abundance of flexibility and time. Make the childless tía your greatest resource. Her childlessness is a gift, and one that must be cherished. Trust that she probably wants to be involved in the lives of the children in your family; she just does not want that involvement to include shame. And more importantly, we cannot tell what someone's body is going to do. Just because someone does not struggle with fertility does not mean their children will also not struggle with fertility. Stop assuming fertility of your children. And stop walking them toward an unpromised destination. Start giving them the option to dream of futures that are not focused on what their wombs can and cannot do.

To the childless tía, what I hope for you is peace with a side of passionate fury. I hope you allow yourself to feel angry about how you were raised to have these expectations of childbearing. But sit with your anger, and may it ignite indignation within you. I hope you start to push your friends and family who are raising girls to think about how the expectation of motherhood is not a promise, but simply one possibility. Fill your girls with purpose, and that includes giving them choices, not a well of motherhood meant to drown them if they don't become mothers themselves. Instill in them a will to dream and the courage to pursue those dreams, whatever they may be. But give them a range of options; they will thank you for it. I hope in being a desvergüenza you can continue to displace the shame meant for you when you clearly do not deserve it. You have nothing to feel ashamed about.

13

THE "TE ESTÁS ENGORDANDO" TÍA

Whatever our size, many of us have been trained to see it as a choice and to see fatness as an irresponsible and immoral one.

—Aubrey Gordon

WHILE MANY OF THESE OTHER TÍAS ARE NOT SOMEONE YOU WOULD think of through that archetype exclusively, this particular tía is someone whose comments on your body are all you remember about her. Her comments reflect a culture of normalized fatphobia, and it is just the spoken reminder that dares to say the thing you fear everyone is thinking—because we have been taught to think of fatness as bad.

The "te estás engordando" tía goes out of her way to police your body and the bodies of all the women in your family. Whenever everyone gathers, her greeting is not the typical "¿Cómo estás?" or even a heartwarming "Te ves alegre." This tía will instead size you up and tell you that you have gained weight. Even if you have not, she has nominated herself as the arbiter of this body-monitoring. Regardless of her own size, she will say this with gusto and even some misdirected disgust. How does this tía look? You might think she herself is slender to brandish such body-shaming without any regard. But because bodies are genetically determined, and all families seem to have this tía among them, she actually has various presentations. She can be thin, or even straight-sized, but she can be in a larger body too. Her own size is not a reflection of what she looks like on the outside, but rather of what she has going on inside, and it reflects often in how she speaks to herself and other women.

I can tell you with rich details about the first time this criticism was directed at me, and even the most recent time it happened to me. This is the thing about the "te estás engordando" tía's behavior: it stays with you. Fatphobia is haunting, and we first internalize it within our own hatred for our changing bodies. This type of body-monitoring feels a bit like Michel Foucault's panopticon. Foucault talks about this way of monitoring people; nation-states do this, though this is a philosophy of surveillance in which we become arbiters of empires even when it does not do us any good. This sense of being seen, of being hypervisible, and this paranoia, is all part of the game of fatphobia and how it is ingrained in us. Fatphobia is happening all around us, and these instances are simply reminders that even when we are functioning outside these spaces, we are still being watched and told to be smaller at every turn.

Yet even when we are the desirable size, it seems that this gaze is here to also tell you to watch out because falling from "grace" is bound to happen. I was fourteen years old the first time my "te estás engordando" tía told me I was getting fat. I remember how shocking it was to become eerily aware of my body in a way I had not been before. I was visiting Nicaragua for spring break and hanging out with my cousins without thinking much about what I looked like. I was just having fun and enjoying every moment with family. And then this tía looked me up and down and told me, "Te estás poniendo gordita." I suddenly felt really bodily aware and every cell in my body felt like it was woken up. I also turned that critique back on her because I was just a kid, and instead of calling what she was doing fatphobia and hoping to have an insightful conversation, I reacted like a cornered cat and told her, "Mira quien está hablando." I should note that I was a small-framed fourteen-year-old, and this remark was clearly meant to chip away at me and make me aware of something. Maybe it was how she was reminding me to stay aware of myself and my gender, or maybe it was a power move; regardless, it was a check. It was meant to do what it did, which was bring me to my knees. This remark was meant to make me aware of myself because to her, I was almost a woman; to her, I was too carefree for my impending shift in status. The comment was meant to remind me of the thing that I have yet to forget: my desirability is my duty.

Thinness can be seen as a defining element of contemporary dominant femininity.

—Justin Charlebois

I was being perceived as grown enough to start my daily audition to the male gaze. I was being tasked with growing up, in that instance, and starting my quest for a man. Maybe I was having too much fun; maybe I was acting too confident; maybe something about me threatened this tía to the extent that she felt the need to remind me of the rules: be pretty and shut the fuck up, where thin equates to pretty. Maybe I had not sucked my stomach in enough for this tía's liking, and because she was the self-nominated male gaze enforcer, she had to let me know that I was existing too comfortably in my own skin, unlike her, a proper woman. A proper woman so preoccupied with being thin and appearing desirable that you cannot even think about breathing too comfortably.

That day, I was wearing a green fitted polo and khaki bell-bottom pants. I remember where I was standing, in front of my abuelita's portón on the sidewalk. I remember how long my hair was. I remember looking down at my body for what felt like the first time.

The most recent time this happened to me was two years ago. Like I mentioned before, everyone is a tía and prima to someone, and tías and primas are not always people we are related to. I do not have a relationship with my criticona tía; my body-shaming tía is not someone I seek to visit because I do not have the energy to be body-checked and keep silent. I can be kind, but learning to soothe myself when I am triggered through body-shaming is more work than I care to do casually. But I did go visit a wonderful friend of mine. When I hang out with her, it feels like I am hanging out with my primas and tías.

I have been in recovery for disordered eating since 2018, and I had finally gained a healthy amount of weight. However, the last time I had seen this friend, I was still living with my restrictive behaviors around food, and so she knew me as someone who barely ate and looked like it. Part of recovery is constantly daring to have a neutral relationship with your body, despite its size. We are not always meant to love our bodies. Society does not give us that freedom, but to actively stop hating it is a huge step in recovery. It is also a fat liberation–centric stance, to see that fat bodies are worthy of love and not shame. If I can be kind to myself, then I can be kind to others.

I remember driving to my friend's house, pulling into her driveway, and texting her that I had arrived. I was trying not to get out of the car in case I happened to have ended up in the wrong driveway, so I waited there. Then I saw the front door fling open, and my friend's face came into clear view. I remember screaming and flinging my car door open and running to her. It was a reunion of sorts, and it felt beautiful to see an old friend.

Then I told her how beautiful her house was and began asking her questions about herself, and she cut me off and said, "Estás más gordita." And just like that, I was transported back to fourteen-year-old me. Here I was, simply existing, and here was another tía/prima ensuring that I remembered the diet panopticon. I am older now; I know that the solution is not to throw back an equally body-monitoring retort. I am not a scared cat. By then I had enough therapy under my belt to understand my fight response. Sometimes people who love us harm us because they are not healing, and it takes a lot of grace toward yourself and them to sit with the harm and not let it destroy your day.

That day I was wearing black leggings and a turtleneck with an oversize coat since it was fall and the weather was cooler. I remember these details. I remember how love and happiness were shat on. I remember the smell in the air, and I remember how someone I care about tried to make me feel.

Our bodies are believed to be meritocracies, direct reflections of the work we're willing to put in. We are expected to judge ourselves on what we're told are the objective measures of our bodies, and we are reminded that others will judge us based on our bodies too.

—Aubrey Gordon

Sometimes understanding that we live in a culture that shames women with bigger bodies means being brave enough to do something about it. By centering my experiences as someone who is in a straight size, I am simply attempting to name the elephant in the room. But this issue affects fat people way more than it could ever affect people in straight sizes. Someone who is straight-sized can easily find their size in any malls and in Ross, Target, and the like. While we are all body-monitored, fat people are the ones who experience the direct oppression that our silence helps create.

What needs to happen in these moments, these moments when we are watching someone normalize fatphobia and allowing it to take root in our ways of thinking, is that we must take that information and investigate it. A snide and equally fatphobic retort might make you feel good in the moment, but it does not alleviate the harm that is done at a systemic level when we allow fatphobia to exist unchallenged.

This is not simply about one or two tías saying something offhandedly that people may learn to shrug off; this is about a normalized system of oppression that specifically targets fat people. Fatphobia results in bad medical care because of weight-biased teaching in medical schools across the board. Fatphobia results in the social policing of fat people because weight biases are normalized. Fat people are less likely to get raises at their jobs, more likely to be filmed in public without their consent, and constantly shamed by people who "mean well." We have equated fatness with moral badness, and then we have let that seep into every part of our world with the moral superiority of our "te estás engordando" tía. We have all become her, even when we can all agree she is wrong for having this attitude. We all worry when we go up a size—we fixate.

The majority of women are a size fourteen and above, and yet we have made clothing for those bodies ugly and hard to find. That is fatphobia. We do not care about fat people as a collective, and our entire society reflects that. And worse yet, we feel angry that this tía reflects a culture we are very willingly complicit in.

But this cultural insistence that fatness is a choice isn't about the veracity of that claim: it's about minimizing fat people's experiences, dismissing our needs, and perpetuating anti-fat bias.

—Aubrey Gordon

When we are told by someone to diet, we learn to fight with that particular person, and we make it a personal dispute between two people. We internalize this as a one-on-one squabble, and we defend our individual right to exist when it is so much bigger than us.

We have let this mentality worm itself into our lives. We say that we do not think this way, but we have inevitably believed the diet panopticon because everything around us says that thinness is better. Tell me when you last saw a person on the *Bachelor* or *Bachelorette* who was bigger than a size six or the equivalent of that for a male contestant; tell me the last time you saw a television show with a fat lead who was not making herself the butt of the jokes. We only want to see fat people on our screens when they are dieting, extreme dieting, and otherwise we prefer thinness.

Thinness is aspirational. Thinness has become code for whiteness and wealth. And there are reasons for that—deeply racist and classist reasons. And we can spit in the face of assimilationist propaganda all day, but when we internalize anti-fat bias, it's nothing but spit with shoddy commitment, at best.

The "te estás engordando" tía is not an insular problem that needs to be dealt with individually. She is a bud sitting on a vast root system that we all participate in.

Like structures that privilege whiteness, cultural and social structures privilege the thin, or at least what has been deemed a "normal"-sized body. Classical social-psychological research indicates that beauty functions as a visible status cue that operates in a similar manner as race or gender and shapes expectations about an individual's personality and behavior.

—Samantha Kwan

And the world is changing—slowly, yes, but it is changing. More and more fat people are embracing a fat liberation stance, daring to believe that they deserve love and proper medical care. But go to the comment section of any public fat person who is not actively dieting, and you will see what society has ultimately taught us about fat people. We have equated being fat with being unhealthy when that stuff can be measured, and you cannot tell someone's blood pressure simply by looking at them. You cannot tell someone's cholesterol levels by looking at them. In fact, you also cannot tell if someone is predisposed to diabetes by just looking at them. We know all these things, and yet we insist that all of those things look like fat people, and then we decide to blame them for something they probably cannot change. And we have disregarded the simple fact that thin people have high blood pressure, thin people experience high cholesterol, and thin people can have diabetes.

We are not all meant to be a size four, or even a straight size. We are diverse in body shapes and sizes, and we always have been. We have different races, different contexts, different diets, and yet we all want to look like the thin white women who have been shoved down our throats via the media. And this is a disservice to all of us who are not white and upper middle class.

Scholars have identified the United States as the country in which the pro-thin, anti-fat bias was gaining strength among elite, morally upright white Americans (especially women) by the nineteenth century and crystallized into a mainstream position by the early twentieth century.

—Sabrina Strings

Only when we stop worshipping at the feet of whiteness can we truly be free. But that shit takes a lot of work; it takes undoing years of socializing, and the "te estás engordando" tía shows us it is easier to get upset at an individual person than to investigate what it all means. Getting comfortable with being uncomfortable about what we have believed to be factual is hard. I have battled this for years and still find myself seeing snippets of my long-standing biases creeping into my psyche. But I insist on thinking and moving differently.

To the family of the "te estás engordando" tía, do we dare start questioning how often we have believed what this tía says? Do we dare to admit that she reflects the diet culture we also participate in? Does this mirror feel too imposing? Does this reality make you angry enough? Because it makes me angry as fuck, and I want better for us, but that all starts when we start to actually care about people in bigger bodies. That all starts when we divest from diet culture and start eating without guilt. That all starts when we stop being afraid of gaining weight.

To the tía who admonishes you for existing, I hope you learn that you deserve love at any size. And I know that is not going to be easy. It sounds easy, and we can intellectualize it till our ears bleed. We can discuss it, and we can say we care about it all, and yet we will contemplate skipping dinner if we've eaten a large lunch.

I repeat, I hope you learn that you deserve love at any size because I hope more of us dare to stop investing so much time, effort, and money into making ourselves smaller. My hope for you is that you can relinquish your commitment to dieting so that more of us can grow up with less-intrusive thoughts around food and gaining weight. If we are so obsessed with being healthy yet we commit to unhealthy habits in the name of thinness, then it is obvious that health is not the goal— thinness is.

So when we admit the truth of what is happening, when we admit it to ourselves, maybe we will create a new world order where tolerating fatphobia is a thing of the past. May we clutch our pearls at this current state of affairs; may we be shocked that we were ever cruel enough to send children to fat camps; may we dare to focus on real health and not the imagined picture of "healthy" that we have learned to see as thin.

I think the lessons here are vast, but know that this tía is not the problem—we all are.

14

BOOK-SMART PRIMA

We knew we were different, set apart, exiled from what is considered "normal," white-right. And we internalized this exile, we came to see the alien within us and too often, as a result, we split apart from ourselves and each other. Forever after we have been in search of that self, that "other" and each other.

—Cherríe Moraga

THE BOOK-SMART PRIMA SLOUCHES, HUNCHED OVER A NEW BOOK AS SHE gets engulfed by it. The book-smart prima will specifically love to read. As she gets into her teenage years, she might stop playing with the other cousins and opt to read instead. For a bit, you might even forget she is around at family gatherings because she disappears to your abuelita's room and stays there reading the entire time.

She will read at both the most opportune and inopportune times. She will be reading when the tías all get together without the kids, but she somehow came along because her mami could always trust she would entertain herself with a book.

She will also be reading when her papi buys the entire family tickets to go see a baseball game, like that time the Marlins made the playoffs, and she sat in her seat reading while her papi looked at her with contempt wondering how she was not appreciating all the money he spent for them to have this experience.

People who do not read, people who do not love to read, will think she is inconsiderate and wonder if something is wrong with her. People who do not read but want to read more will think she is gifted for having the bandwidth to sit and concentrate on a book.

She will manage to disconnect when everyone else is connecting.

The book-smart prima's mami will tell the other tías that she took the book-smart prima to the biblioteca, and she checked out ninety-nine books. "Lo máximo que se puede sacar!" she will exclaim with a mixture of excitement and terror. The other tías will raise their eyebrows, impressed and wondering if your tía is lying. Surely they have all seen her read, but no kid reads that fast or makes it through that many books in a lifetime. Yet this prima does, and she will continue to read regardless of whether they believe it to be true or not; she loves books and cannot get enough of them.

She is different. And I do not mean this in a way that creates hierarchies among women. She is just like the other primas but different in that when books become someone's guiding light, they begin to reflect those teachings. Family is oftentimes who we reflect; we reflect their teachings, and they imprint culture onto us through our constant exposure to them. But if you are a reader, you have an additional teacher—an additional reflection to imprint onto you.

She might introduce the entire group of cousins to Chinese jump rope because she read about it in a book. She might love playing out storylines from her favorite new novel. She will also begin to speak differently. She is going to be exposed to new words, bigger words, and she will test them out with family. Often, she will be mispronouncing words, words she has never heard said but discovered through reading them. And no one can correct her because it is all new to all of them. In being first, you sort of have to be willing to try new things. Fearless.

She is different because she is going to be asking questions and pushing forward in a way that is mostly self-guided. That is going to make her different. Not better, but different. And this distinction is important because soon she will feel different within herself, and the outside world will tell her that makes her better. So much of this prima's journey is rooted in her ability to come back home and away from that belief. She will need to learn to travel to these worlds she is discovering in her books and then turn around and return to her own home.

As outsiders to the mainstream, women of color in the United States practice "world"-traveling, mostly out of necessity.

—Maria Lugones

To be on the book-smart prima's journey is a lonely experience. The book-smart prima may also be referred to as the prima of *firsts*. According to a Pew study conducted in 2022, eight out of ten Latines in the USA do not have a bachelor's degree. According to that same study, 71 percent of Latines do not go to college because they say that they are helping support their families. And it is often hard to find bookish community members among Latines since often the book-smart primes may be the only ones reaching high academic achievements, not just within their immediate family units but in their entire church communities and neighborhoods. They have to find one another in colleges and universities. I can name everyone I grew up with who is a high achiever in academia because, you know, you remember who "got out," and we see one another across the various states and countries we have all ended up in, away from our homes. A *first* knows very intimately who else is a *first* from their contexts.

> *A large body of social science research indicates… that Latino/a, African American, and Native American students have lower rates of college enrollment and retention than white students.*
>
> —Angela Harris

Even the language used to describe the experience of a "*first*" is often clouded with class and racial biases, such as "got out," "made it," "overachiever," "special," or "gifted." And if unchecked, this thinking will create a further divide for those who do get to step into these elite and exclusive spaces not made for us. There is this displacement that happens when you are a *first*, which if you are an immigrant becomes compounded, a double displacement. You are a foreigner in the new lands you migrated to and a foreigner among your family when you become the first among them to get a bachelor's degree, master's degree, or doctorate. You learn all this new terminology and live in a world that your family has no real access to other than through you.

> *Underrepresented students of color also report higher levels of stress and anxiety, caused partly by straitened economic circumstances and partly by the alienating environment of predominantly white institutions.*
>
> —Angela Harris

While the book-smart prima's awareness at a young age will be about knowing what the adults in the room already learned, at some point she may surpass them. To the book-smart prima and those who meet her within her family's community, this knowingness she will move with is going to make her difference feel off-putting to some. In our cultura, knowledge is important, like knowing a good mechanic or having a friend with a plug to a nurse or a pharmacist who you can call when you're worried about an emergency hospital visit. Overall, knowing who to know is lifesaving. Her type of book knowledge is going to feel unnecessary for the daily lives of her family, and maybe even scary. She is going to start feeling unfamiliar, and in this she will potentially feel less like her family and more like a white person.

That is not to say that white people are all book-smart, or that they are the only ones capable of becoming smart. In fact,

I do not believe that to be true based on my own experiences with whiteness. Rather, when systemic oppression is the lay of the land, there are substantive obstacles that stand in the way of being the best we can be—and so because of that, when we observe someone act in ways we have only seen people in power act—people who oftentimes are white and wealthy—we take note. You cannot help but make the associations you see around you.

> *Becoming white meant gaining access to a whole set of public and private privileges that materially and permanently guaranteed basic subsistence needs and, therefore, survival. Becoming white increased the possibility of controlling critical aspects of one's life rather than being the object of other's domination.*
>
> —Kimberlé Crenshaw

At some point the book-smart prima will start college, and she might not study something practical; she might want to study something she loves. She might be encouraged to do this, or she might fight with her parents and study something she loves regardless of their opinions. But she will pursue something that she will do excellently. She is a top student, an honors student, with a lot of scholastic accolades. She will become someone her mami brags about, but not too much.

At the beginning, things will feel like they have always felt, like the book-smart prima is different but the same. But it is at this point in her education where things will begin to shift. You will start to notice that she is actually not present at all the family functions. The cousins might search for her in the abuelita's bedroom, surprised to not find her buried in a book. She may move to continue to attend school for longer than anyone ever has in the family, so distance begins to play a factor in how connected she continues to be. You might occasionally see her for holidays, but that will soon also die down. But being around other book-smart people at the academic level where she is means she might feel like she is finding her people.

Her graduations become large affairs with everyone in the family gathering. And at first, it will be exciting. But at some point, everyone will wonder, "¿Y qué está estudiando ahora?" as they fumble through pronouncing her next degree. Everyone keeps wondering how this will help the family, how this will advance all their futures, and she will have no answers for that because this is a lonely road with few advantages for a village. It is a privileged place, academia, and often those who make it into those spaces can afford to be selfish and think endlessly and talk about what they are thinking with no goal in sight.

In a certain respect, being working-class and becoming an academic is an oxymoron. Academics aspire to genteel, professional success; working-class life rejects the genteel for the overt—at times even rude—acknowledgement that life is difficult. Academics revel in a world of carefully chosen words and phrases; subtlety and indirection are prized. A well-delivered, witty repartee at a party is always rewarded. At a working-class party, it would be much safer to say exactly what you mean in a direct way.

—Constance G. Anthony

Those who are supposed to make it into those spaces are not supposed to bring entire family units there, like opening a business where you can employ your family members. This is a solo career, and the benefits are for one and maybe some younger generations of children who may then aspire to such a path. Knowledge is power, but it will not pay all your family's bills. Academia is an elite career path meant for white straight men with family wealth supporting their lives of the production of knowledge. Because publishing does not pay academics well, they are often encouraged to write for free, for the sake of knowledge, for the sake of saying something important without compensation as the driving force, instead being driven by a will to expand their own minds and the minds of their peers. And that all sounds noble, or whatever, but ultimately if you are a first, this does nothing to help your family and oftentimes does little to even help that first-generation student. What's notoriety if you are living paycheck to paycheck? What's low-profile academic fame if the only ones benefitting are other academics reading your work?

As a *first*, though, the book-smart prima's people in academic spaces will statistically not come from Latine households, and so she will speak English more and start to stumble in her Spanish. She is finding that others "like" her, and the more she spends time with them the less time she will spend with her family. She is being displaced and integrated into a whole other space, a whole other world. As a *first*, she quickly becomes an island, and she may have no time to actually notice what is happening all around her. Her circles are shrinking while her new world seems to be expanding. The dissonance in all of that will feel suffocating.

Depending on her field of study, she may start talking about what she does when she visits her family. The men in the family, the ones who think of themselves as clever, may take interest in her, and they may ask her questions. What they will know will be valuable but not in the traditional academic sense, and she might brush them off. If she is able, she will try to be gentle and kind in explaining what she does. But if she is tired and stretched thin and accustomed to the fight that graduate studies normalize, she may be short and easily frustrated when folks do not comprehend what she so easily understands. Either way, the shift of environments between school and home starts to feel too drastic, and you might stop seeing her altogether.

> *Being nurturing and humble does not translate well into the competitive academic cultural environment, so adapting mandates some cultural retooling for many of us.*
>
> —Linda Trinh Vo

She may lose herself in her new friend circles. She may keep going to school and become part of the unicorn club, part of a group of *firsts*. A Latine with a doctoral degree is rare, and to reach that goal means a level of devotion and sacrifice that few can comprehend. If she climbs that mountain, if she survives the hurdles created for her, her family will most likely not understand what she does and find themselves unable to even begin to wrap their minds around it all. The graduation party at the end of that journey will have more friends than family, and it will be small. Isolation may have been a reason she is able to earn this highly unattainable degree, but it has trimmed her circles, and her worlds may feel oceans apart.

Her parents might ask, and then complain to the family often, about why their hija is always busy. They do not understand that as a minoritized person in academia, she has to carry a lot on her plate and then some. They do not understand that she needs to fight to stay in the game. They do not understand her at all. And soon enough, she may begin to fully realize how small her world has become when for a while it felt so expansive. She will find herself struggling with what her "home" is when she has been away from it for so long.

One of the most energy-draining aspects of being on the margins is the constant requirement to justify your existence: why are you here?

—Stephanie A. Shields

She will attempt to explain what she does to her mami, all while seeking tenure and carrying out research and writing. All while teaching and attempting to mentor other minoritized students like herself. She will try to clarify that it is not that she does not value family, but that it is all drowning her. And then her mami will say, "Este año vente para las navidades" like she did not hear her. What the book-smart prima is attempting to do is to create a bridge for her mami to cross over to her. And with a sigh of release, the book-smart prima will oblige after years of missing out. At this point, when the piles of work do not seem to get trimmed down regardless of how much she tries, she will resign herself to at least making her mami happy.

Traveling to each other's "worlds" would enable us to be through loving each other.

—Maria Lugones

Walking back into her family home, she will feel something she has not felt in years. There will be this moment during that long-awaited visit when she will realize, as she stares at the tías gossiping and the new generation of primas playing, that she has been missing something. Things will start to sink in, and she will find herself relieved that she came. She will realize that while she was trying to build a bridge for her mami to come to her, her mami had already built a bridge for her to come back home. What she had been missing was her home and the people who shaped her into who she is today. She will also realize that she has built a new home with her new community of firsts.

She will be reminded that while she focused hard in her struggle toward becoming a *first*, she lost something along the way. She lost a crucial part of herself when she lost her community of kin, even when she gained so many new and wonderful things among chosen family. She will find inspiration in being with her family.

Being with them might even begin to fuel her research like never before. She will eventually realize that her opportunities simply were not reflective of the ones all her other primas had because, at some point, she was seen as "special." Sometimes a teacher picks you as a favorite, which means you were doted on by a mentor-like figure. Sometimes the way we dress signals our goodness. Sometimes not cussing signals worthiness. And maybe your other primas did not know how to signal goodness in ways that whiteness expects goodness to feel, sound, look, and so on. Realizing that it is not exceptional intelligence that leads to opportunities, and that often it is about class and class perception, will lead to resenting the very institutions you spent years trying to create a home within.

To the book-smart prima's family, home should feel inviting. I invite you all to see the ways that we can create more warmth for those younger generations looking to pave new paths toward new goals and destinations. Encourage your children to pursue what makes them happy, and they will surprise you in what they will come up with. But mostly, offer words of encouragement as your children become firsts in spaces you may not understand. They need all the support they can get.

To the book-smart prima, the beauty in being a *first* is when those realizations start to hit you. When that one white male professor lets slip that he grew up with more access to favorable outcomes for his future because both of his parents were dentists or doctors or lawyers, you realize that you might not have as much in common with your more educated peers than you do with your family. The beauty of that realization ultimately begins to readjust your own perception of your academic experiences. Your ability to navigate spaces that are uninviting to your kind of people is a talent; give yourself breaks to breathe and exist not as a world traveler but as a daughter, a cousin, an aunt, a woman, a lover, a friend.

Remember that home is not in institutions that want you placid, with your head down, and making them money while taking all their collusion with this empire without so much as a sigh. Home is not exclusive and hard-to-get-into spaces; rather, it should be spaces that feel warm, where everyone should be welcomed. Home is intentional, and you will see it when it falls into place. One day, you will find yourself in the family gathering, chatting with your fellow tías because your primas have all become parents, and you'll smile as you see the one prima reading her books in this abuelita's bedroom. Home is where you are free and happy to do just that.

As the book-smart prima, I have had to learn that I am not smarter than folks without the same educational level that I have attained. I knew how to perceive systems and navigated them in ways that benefitted my book-smart goals. I knew adults expected goodness from me, and I learned to perform it for my benefit. I also knew that adults could be assholes and learned to navigate that too. Understanding that internalized biases mean people will create barriers to your success based on those biases means also acknowledging that opportunities are not created equal. Learning all of this was my ultimate mountain, and at the peak of this mountain, I found myself in my natural habitat. I found home in the chosen family I met in graduate school. Among a sea of whiteness, there were specks of color that changed my entire universe. Those specks became my entire world; I became engulfed by them. I found home in people who love who I really am at my core.

15

DIVORCED TÍA

Purity culture teaches that preserving a marriage relationship, once it has been created, is the highest priority for Christians. Longevity is virtually equated with success and the ending of a relationship is a failure. No matter what happens, you must protect your marriage.

—Emily Joy Allison

THIS TÍA GOT MARRIED YOUNG, AS MANY IN MY FAMILY ARE ENCOURAGED to do, and was divorced young too. She has never pursued another significant relationship, meaning she has never introduced anyone to the family. These people never meet the family, probably for good reasons in a family where everything is up for discussion. She will leave the house to meet people at the corner of the street, so we all know she occasionally dates, because she makes herself scarce. But then through the passage of time, they disappear, and she moves on, seemingly unperturbed.

She had a child out of the acceptable, prepackaged life plan of marriage and never got remarried, but she carries a shame that she disguises with disinterest, and there is more to her distance. There is always more to their distance. It is as though she feels like a burden.

This tía is proud, like pride has more value to her than most things. She has learned to protect her pride from probing eyes and ears. She does not share much, and she never fakes enthusiasm for anything she is not genuinely excited about. She is principled.

This tía is the butt of jokes in the childhood stories mi mami tells, and when you are at your baddest, your mami tells you that you remind her of her sister. Mi mami would warn me through gritted teeth, encouraging me to be more like her and less like the sister who grew up to be single and a mother. It is clear as day, and it is revolting to process that in all its intricacies.

It is absurd how normal it is to make her life appear to be the consequence of bad decisions, of a bad character. You start to think that maybe this is why they fight behind closed doors, because your mami might say even worse things behind them.

The link between divorce and purity culture is clear. Purity culture is the overemphasis of obtaining and protecting heterosexual relationships, regardless of the detrimental effect that relationship may have on women and the children in these dynamics. And so, while divorce has a lot of elements that should and can be discussed, it is perceived "chosen singleness" that is truly the issue here. In some significant ways, this archetype includes single mothers who never married because the implications are the same: they had a man, and they do not have a man anymore, and they are somehow to blame for that very detail.

Whether Christian or not, Latines have absorbed purity culture with reckless abandon. And purity culture demands marriages remain intact—for life.

> *Purity culture is not just a self-reinforcing system but a self-policing one.*
>
> —Emily Joy Allison

My divorced tía falls asleep to the radio, with the volume cranked up, like loudness is comforting to her. She sleeps alone in a huge bed with her arms stretched out above her head and her legs sprawled out. The level of commitment to her sleep paired with the loudness of her radio is actually fascinating. I can picture it clearly; I have seen this image hundreds of times while I slept in the top bunk of the bunk bed next to her bed. Whenever we visited and spent the night, I stayed in her room. She is single, and even though she is older than my parents, she is not afforded the privacy that married couples automatically get when the family gathers. Singleness robs her of privacy that is only reserved for married couples, the real adults.

I cannot for the life of me fall asleep to her loud radio, but I wouldn't dare tell her to shut it off. This tía does not signal that she is open to dialogue about anything, but rather that she will do whatever she wants to do whenever she is able to do it. Her child is her only priority, and that is felt in the ways she manages her time and her availability or lack thereof.

She has created spaces for herself to feel safe, to feel alive, or maybe just to keep her own thoughts at bay. This tía is quiet too. She will give you all her attention when it is just you and her, but with other people and with your parents, she silently observes. Leaning back on her chair often, with both hands crossed in front of her, waiting. It is like she knows something you do not know, or she has been through something that she will not burden anyone with, but whatever she has gone through, it has managed to stay with her. It feels like it is in every room with her, in every glare that seems to speak a thousand words, though not a single one escapes her lips. She is always thinking; you can see it in her eyes.

And it is not that she does not speak. I have heard through my mami that they disagree and argue and get into heated debates, but I have never witnessed those conversations. We were always shielded from those discussions, which is rare. We are a family that openly speaks and openly critiques except when it comes to specific vices. Adults do not talk about our alcoholic uncle in front of children, and whatever is being discussed with this tía is also spoken in hushed tones.

The ultimate symbol that a woman has successfully embodied hegemonic femininity is securing a nonplatonic heterosexual relationship.

—Justin Charlebois

Maybe this tía stopped trying to make herself into whatever the other women in our family needed to justify their own decisions to stay in loveless marriages. Maybe this tía is just wiser than all the others and has learned to create boundaries without naming them but always honors her boundaries to herself. Maybe we all have something to learn here, smiling our plastered bravado without tending to the pain others may have caused us. Maybe we are not prepared for the pain; we are not prepared to see that pain for what it is, and this tía has made a point to stay prepared.

Maybe this tía is all of us, going through tough times with wide-eyed, impressionable children staring and wondering why she feels so *different* than other adults.

As I have gotten older, I have picked up more pieces to the puzzle—more pieces that make it all make sense and get me even angrier at how my tía was treated.

My tía got married young to a good-looking man. I have seen photographic evidence. He was a looker, and my tía looked happy. My uncle fought in our civil war in the Sandinista army. He went missing in action for long enough that many began to assume he had died, only to reappear a shadow of himself many months later. He was in Cuba when he went missing. Upon his return, he came back with a nifty little new addiction: alcoholism.

Alcoholism and PTSD oftentimes go hand in hand, especially when the country you fought to defend does nothing to help you. My uncle survived a war but lost something while fighting. Soon after his return, this tía packed up her things and moved back into her own mother's home. She took back her old childhood bedroom, got a reliable job, and took care of her little family. She was determined not to become her mother's responsibility, but rather to take ownership of what was hers and do it well. She does not like asking for help, never did. It is important to her that she not need help because asking for it reminds her of what everyone makes her feel is missing in her life. She does not need that reminder, a reminder she is trying to undo by being self-reliant.

For generations women accepted the role of legitimizing humans through marriage to a man. They agreed that a human was not acceptable unless a man said so. Without that "masculine" protection, the mother is vulnerable.

—Clarissa Pinkola Estés

I have this tía who loves differently, engages differently, and most importantly shows you that being detached from people who are critical of your life is sometimes a smart tactic. We do not have to allow people to be mean to us, and we do not owe them our vulnerability when they are quick to throw salt into a wound.

I myself got divorced and became single again in my thirties, and while I did not have children, I feared telling my parents. I was a full-blown adult who did not financially rely on them, and still I feared them. I grew up with purity culture rammed down my throat, and my relationship with my parents was not one of open communication. Where men were concerned, in any romantic sense, I was taught shame until marriage—and if that marriage dissolves, then the shame is mandatorily reinstated.

I remember calling mi mami to tell her I had left my ex-husband. I made sure that I was no longer living with my ex when I revealed my "tragedy" to them, this failure. I understood that the shame would keep me in the marriage, and not my own shame, but rather the borrowed shame of my parents. And so first I left, and then I made that phone call.

When I did, my mami could not believe the betrayal (to her personally) that I had committed. She reminded me of my wedding vows, and how we had made a commitment to God. She was not interested in my reasoning, and when I told her why I had to leave, she said I was lying. To her the reason for breaking such weighty vows had to be very specific. My life had to be in danger, and only that justified this level of shame I was bringing down on my entire family.

> *Purity culture teaches that preserving a marriage relationship, once it has been created, is the highest priority…Longevity is virtually equated with success and the ending of a relationship is a failure.*
>
> —Emily Joy Allison

Within purity culture, leaving men is never an option unless it is between life and death. In my parents' church's perspective, the dilemma here was my ruin. I was believed to have remained "pure" till my marriage day. It was my mami's testimony that I had done right by them, and I let her believe that because admitting otherwise would mean more shame. I carried enough shame to allow my parents to dump some more of that shame on me, so I silently stood aside as she bragged about her parenting skills as reflected in my hymen.

It is sick.

So when I became single again, what they understood is that my hymen was no longer intact. My purity, the modern-day dowry paid by my parents to any man, was now gone, as they understood it. It is all very heterosexual and suffocating. I experienced purity culture to be as such. I remember the weight on my chest when I hung up on my mami mid-conversation, mid-beratement. This was the shame I was avoiding while trying to decide whether I should leave or stay. This was the shame that could have kept me in that marriage, till death did we part.

I thought I had strategized sufficiently, but her words haunted me. I cried endlessly. I could only avoid their shame for so long. And I even went back to the marriage I had left, briefly. The shame of purity culture will stuff you in the neat boxes they created for us and leave us to suffer—but at least we remain honorable.

Returning to my ex-husband only made the ordeal longer, and I know I only ended up hurting us more. But purity culture demanded it, and I bowed down again.

I was raised to believe certain "truths" about my worth as a woman. Because that is the thing about purity culture: it has disguised itself as honorable and therefore truer than any other truth out there. Defying this "truth" meant that I was "lying" to myself—that is how fucked those narratives are and how embedded it all becomes. Not only did it mean that I was "lying" to myself by leaving and thinking I could be okay, but it meant "lying" to others.

I remember that when I started to date, I opted quickly to not tell anyone about my divorce. I also opted to not share with my family much about whom I was dating. I kept my worlds separate. I rarely told anyone I was divorced. I learned to keep that to myself because the people I went on dates with were quick to show disgust or disdain for what was assumed to be a less innocent life. Not only was mi mami correct about her assessment that I was "ruined," but attempting to date confirmed it in so many ways. It took me a bit to learn not to hide that part of myself.

There are parts of my divorced tía that I carried and still carry with me. I carry the scars of being treated like you are ruined by your own family. If I had not made concerted efforts to heal those scars, I can see how self-reliance would have been a viable solution. I can see how learning to silence the voices in my head through loud music would feel peaceful. I did that too. I do that too. I learned to distract myself in my journey toward healing, but healing is not linear. Years of a specific type of rearing, with the rod, means that some days I am managing and other days I am distressed. I learned to disassociate from my own intrusive thoughts until I could manage those voices telling me of my worthiness. I know better, but the loudness makes it bearable for when I do not have the energy to silence those negative thoughts.

I have not seen my divorced tía since before I even got married. While there is tenderness I carry for her, my own scars make me scared to approach her; my scars make me scared of a lot of things. Fear becomes a guiding force for whom I distribute my tenderness toward. But I want to put my arms around her body to feel like we are carrying together the literal shame we were told to carry alone. Maybe it will feel less lonely to hug her tenderly, like someone who understands a tiny fraction of what she endured from loved ones.

But I also know this tía does not do physical touch well. I do not either. Like her, I have become measured and distant, and it shows in my relationships with my nieces, nephews, and niblings. The things my family said to me amid my divorce stayed with me. But I insist that we heal in community, and I want to heal that with another woman who was told that her shame was hers to carry alone—or else.

To the family of the divorced tía, divorce is usually initiated by women. Statistically, women are not set up for success in marriages, yet we ram that binding agreement down into our psyches and destroy our spirits. And when we are divorced, we are either discouraged from dating—usually if children are involved—or encouraged to remarry after an acceptable amount of time has passed, assuming you have sisters who lead with a purity culture narrative but also have what they presume to be compassion. By encouraging remarrying, you might think you are offering them another chance to get it right. But getting remarried is in no way a signifier of any type of healing because heterosexual marriages are not set up for our success. Do not bind anyone back to a life that may not be for them. And do not confuse being alone with loneliness either.

To the single-mother tía who has never married, doing things in their "wrong order" does not reflect poorly on you; it reflects poorly on how we pressure women to fit into boxes not made for our needs. As if we all need and require the same things to feel connected. You are beautiful and strong and thoughtful, and you do not have to carry any shame attached to the happenstances of life.

To the divorced tía, know that there is nothing wrong with leaving someone who you vowed to love till your dying days. To myself, I sternly say, you need no valid excuse for leaving your husband. Valid through the eyes of purity culture, valid through the judgmental eyes of the church, valid through the judgmental eyes of other men. Know that time will heal wounds, but you have to seek ways to heal too; healing does not occur in isolation but with community. I hope that you see me here, standing and waiting for you to see yourself as I insist on seeing myself—as someone strong enough to know better and do better. Know that many people stay in loveless marriages because of the shame that seems to swallow us whole, and maybe showing them some of our joys will entice them to seek a freer life.

> *In purity culture, marriage is the ultimate goal of human*
> *life and the ultimate state of being.*
> —Emily Joy Allison

We do not have to be extraordinary to justify our leaving. We have to simply exist fully in our decisions, and that is good. The end of our marriages never meant the end of us, but rather the beginning of something new. May we be willing to start anew at any age in life, and at every stage in life. May we be so bold as to dare to believe in ourselves beyond the limitations of purity culture.

16

SECOND MOM TÍA

For women who travel in packs of one.

—Cherríe Moraga

THIS TÍA IS YOUR MAMI'S CLOSEST SISTER, CLOSEST COUSIN, OR EVEN your play tía, which means she is your mami's closest friend who you see as equal to a tía. This tía is someone who you know has your back because she would do anything for your mami, just as your mami would do anything for her and her children. She knows your mami in a way that your mami seldom allows anyone to know her. They are cut from the same cloth because your mami's friend, your second mom tía, is a mystery to most people who encounter her too.

The second mom tía is someone who watches you grow. Her desire to stay an active spectator, watching your evolution into adulthood, makes your bond one that will change through the ages. She may eventually become a confidant because she knows you, but she can offer different insight. She can become a sort of friend to the kids of the woman she is so close to because she is not their mother. When Mami may feel too involved and too opinionated, she feels less tyrannous. In her distance, she provides an alternative perspective that her closeness gives her access to. She will sound like your mami but softer, and maybe more reasonable. She is willing to explain herself where your mami might not always be so willing, and where she may not be so willing if these were her children approaching her.

Aside from who this tía is to your mami, she is someone else entirely to the children in her life. Because what makes this tía especially special is her willingness to care for and love someone else's children like they are her own. This tía can handle fun and lightness, and she can reprimand and correct. Not all adults can reconcile all of that for children that are not theirs. She can embrace the levity of childhood and the correction that must take place when rearing children. And she will not overstep, even when she is told she has free rein. Their trust for one another is tangible in these ways.

> *To love women is, at least in part, to perceive them with loving eyes.*
>
> —Maria Lugones

One of my second mom tías is my mami's little sister. The ways they have chosen to raise their kids and move in the world almost feel synonymous. They are thick as thieves. She is her, her is she. If you squint a little, you may not even realize who is who.

To me, this tía looks the most like my mami, with the same beautiful smile and neck-to-shoulders ratio. They have the same laugh lines, and even their birthmarks are identically placed. They both have wild hair, not curly but not straight, and it is thick. Their hair seems to sit atop their heads in full display like a lion's mane with more texture. And to me, they are my lions and resemble that—mis leonas.

They speak often about their lives, and they consult with each other when they are having issues with their spouses. They are friends, though it took my abuelita dying for this transition to occur. Before that they were sisters, and that bond was special and cannot be overstated. But when mi abuelita died, everyone had to consider their roles in that family. It felt like everyone had to figure out how they were going to function without the matriarch around. Not only that, but those feelings of uncertainty within our family meant that someone had to take the time to explain things to my mami—things she would not be privy to unless she could be there in the same country and in the same city. This tía took it upon herself to gather information and bring my mami into the fold when everyone else was handling their grief and spinning off in different directions trying to find their own North Star now that ours had passed. This tía took the time to explain things to my mami. She took the time to tell her about the tía who came to visit, how their papi/my abuelo Nicolas was doing, and how our uncle's new girlfriend had just moved in. She makes an effort to help mi mami feel less disconnected.

She still takes that time. Recently, mi mami was coming home from El Salvador after my uncle had just passed and my dad went to the funeral to say goodbye to his brother. As they were flying home, they had a short connection in Nicaragua, and so mi mami told her sister that she was going to be flying over her home. The second mom tía looked for a mirror, and then she said she made it reflect in the sun as soon as she saw a plane she suspected was mi mami's. Mi mami shared this while laughing but also because I am sure that it meant a lot to her. She feels the weight of our migration and often wishes to move back to Nicaragua, and through these moments when mi tía attempts to narrow the gap, she feels held and loved. It is tender, and it is a tenderness seldom shared with others. But it is a much-needed type of affection that lets us meet one another's needs without having to ask.

Their personalities are also matched; both of them are loud, and when they are together they get louder. They are easily perceived as introverts outside the safety bubbles they create, but I do not believe them to be introverts because I exist within their bubbles and have only known them to take center stage. Their sense of humor is the same, and their sense of justice is very aligned. When they talk about childhood memories together, they tilt their heads in the same way. Her kids express shock when they face that realization we have all reached at one point or another: "¡Son tan similares!"

Their age difference is significant, and so they did not grow up directly playing together. My mom was more of a second mom to my aunt for most of their respective childhoods. I grew up being taken care of by this aunt, so it all gets jumbled for me since to me they are both adults, but they have always seemed to be the most aware of their age gap. Maybe that is how I will feel about my little sister. To me she is always my little sister, even when she is in her thirties. But also, as she and I age and experience more adulthood together, we bond over how our shared childhoods mean we have similar reflections and instincts about things. My sister and I especially bond over how we were parented, laughing often at our mami's inability to apologize or our brother's tantrums as a grown man. We spend a lot of time reminiscing about the past, like two viejitas, yet we are both in our thirties. That warmth that comes from sharing space with someone so familiar, that is what watching my mami and the second mom tía felt and still feels like today.

Their laughter brings a smile to my face, it's inevitable, because it is that infectious. They have so much fun when they are together that they do not just laugh, they bend over cry-laughing. As a child, I would just sit there with my dolls, watching and smiling. As a little girl, I never understood their jokes, but I never questioned the hilarity of their exchanges. And they would try to include me, but I simply did not understand. Most of what they talk about is the past, and you had to be there to get it, like when they talk about my dad's fashion in the '70s, when he wore his white shiny pleather platform shoes to visit my mom. My dad is a creative, an artist, and he played in a band his entire life. He dressed flashily. I could never picture it even as they described it while trying to catch their breath between laughs. I would laugh along with them because they were laughing, not always because of what they were saying to me. Their memories of our family never felt like the family I knew then or even know today. They had their own special memories, the memories you make when you grow up with someone.

Conversation and social interaction are a major part of women's lives and gesture and voice are crucial to these communications.

—Devra Anne Weber

And as an adult, I don't dare speak when they are flowing so as not to break the palpable magic of their bond. I oftentimes find myself holding my breath and laughing at their jokes a little less intensely so I don't distract from what they are saying to each other. I am a spectator of their joy and a recipient of what that love does to everyone around them. I often say I was taught how to love in Spanish because these were the moments of pure affection that I grew up watching, and I never heard a lick of English mixed in there. Intimacy sounds like Spanish, at my core. Love sounds like Spanish.

I can sink into that feeling. There is a part of me that longs for that feeling. There is a part of me that wants to bottle it and save it for the dark days when the sun cannot shine on me. I want to feel that level of sisterliness close to me. They are each other's beloveds. Their exchanges are anything but important; nothing crucial is being discussed. They are simply recalling their childhood memories together and enjoying the younger versions of themselves. And yet it feels life-giving and life-sustaining. You can see them shed the weight of adulthood around each other. They look lighter, they feel freer.

Migration meant that my second mom tía, my mami's younger sister, was not around on a regular basis due to physical distance and a lack of resources, so we didn't get to see her as often as we would have all preferred. Because of that, my very distrusting mami eventually found a second mom tía for us in Miami. Mi mami found her absolute best friend.

My mami's best friend took her years to cultivate once we migrated. She was Central American like us, so she knew us culturally. She was Guatemalan, specifically. Mi mami even met her family back in Guate! Both mi mami and this friend were stay-at-home moms who had a reputation for being feared. And while all their kids differed in age, her children were significantly younger than us. Her oldest was around my sister's age but younger by a few years. We knew that their friendship was deep and more profound than any other friendship they had. Their friendship reminded us that our mamis were women, and once upon a time they were girls who loved to giggle and especially loved to share worlds. Through their friendship, we get glimpses of our mothers that otherwise elude us all. The responsibility of becoming women, the responsibility of becoming wives, all of that seems to shift things for them in penetratingly obvious ways. And it only becomes that overt when they are together, their shoulders relax, and they become who they once were, or versions of that—glimpses of that.

> *Women's typical body language, [is] a language of relative tension and constriction.*
>
> —Sandra Lee Bartky

I understood this tía to be stern but kind. She held the ability to be liked/loved even when scolding us for being mean or "bad." I remember there was this older man in our church who seemed to love to scream at kids for running. I presume the logic was that we were going to get hurt, but children run and play, and getting hurt is part of the deal. And yes, it can be disruptive, but church spaces are family spaces that include children, and disruption is part of that. I knew he had not been given the authority to rule over me, and so when he yelled at me, I would quickly scan the room to see if my mami was anywhere to be found because if she was, she'd come to my rescue. Only my second mom tía, my papi, and she had that authority. I knew it, they knew, and that man eventually learned it. According to the handbook of parenting as often preached by mi mami, it takes trust to allow someone to tell your children what is right and wrong, and trust is earned, never given.

And if she was nowhere in sight, I would simply ignore him. I knew what it took to be allowed to speak to me like I needed correcting. I knew my mother's mothering enough to know that parenting was her responsibility, not just any adult's; her authority was law and only those she deemed worthy got access to that authority. This tía also knew my mother's mothering and had no interest in changing any of it or creating her own rules for me. She understood my mother's mothering because it was similar to her mothering, and so she brought her kids up the same way. Her love for my mami meant she loved me, and the way she raised me was out of that place of love and not one of wanting to exert power over me just because she could. Some adults parent from that place, and it is felt. A second mom tía teaches you that difference between friends and acquaintances. She keeps you in touch with parts of yourself this world will try to rob from you.

Women more generally are separated from each other by overresponsibility, co-optation, and the horror of female existence. We are separated from each other by ongoing male violence, male-serving ideologies, patriarchal marriage, and the threat of poverty, which helps keep those marriages intact.

—Bonnie Burstow

My second mom tía passed away back when I was in college. She got breast cancer, and it was pretty aggressive the first time, but she got chemo and we saw her go through it all. We watched as she lost her hair; we saw her become half her size; we watched as she started to regrow her hair and come back to life. And then she got it again, just as aggressively, and she was done fighting. The first time had taken all she had, and she insisted on enjoying the moments she had left.

When she eventually passed, my mami helped in any way she could. She went through her clothes with her mother, and they decided what to donate together. Her mother viewed mi mami and her friendship with her daughter as a significant part of her daughter's life and told her so. She viewed my mami with the warmth of someone who understands that they loved your child deeply.

Para una mujer, ser mujer no pasa por la conciencia.

—Marcela Lagarde y de los Ríos

Mi mami has a picture of her best friend in her bathroom, a picture she often looks at when mourning the loss of that great friendship. Mi mami has not found an equally earth-expanding friendship; those types of friendships come once in a lifetime. The second mom tía is your mami's friend first before she is ever anything to any of us. My second mom tía's passing felt like something monstrously enormous was taken from us all. A significant loved one's death leaves a crater behind. My second mom tía is irreplaceable in the ways we think only family is irreplaceable, in the ways only best friends are irreplaceable, in the ways only mamis are irreplaceable. There is simply too much to protect about close female friendships. May we all be lucky to have more than one, but one is still enough when longing for a friend is the alternative.

> *On the geographic level the overall gender separation translates into the dispersion of women into the various homes of the oppressors.*
>
> —Bonnie Burstow

So significant is the bond between your mami and your second mom tía that if she is not related to your mami, she is still treated like family. She receives the high regard that family gets, and she can see past the curtain of what is perceived to what is true within the family. She knows the matriarch; she knows the escandalosa; she knows everyone and is aware of all the family chisme. She has her opinions on it all, but she knows when to share them. She is all-knowing. She knows who to speak to, who to avoid, and how to navigate the minefield found in many family dynamics.

The mami stamp of approval is hard to acquire and hard to maintain, but your second mom tía has it, and everyone knows that means a lot. The reverence their husbands have toward that friendship is perceptible. The husbands are kept on the periphery of their friendship, but the husbands also very much understand that the existence of the other in their wives' lives is significant enough to cause friction between them if they get in the way. Everyone behaves because everyone seems to understand the necessity for the other. In that way, the second mom tía also respects the partnership. Even if she may have her own thoughts about the spouse, she knows to share that in private with the friend. Their friendship allows them to divulge anything and everything to each other; they are each other's safe space, and possibly their only sacred space.

The second mom tía may not hang out a lot with your mom, but they speak often. They are up to date on each other's family affairs. Simply by virtue of hearing their conversations while your mami makes dinner, drives to Marshalls, or goes to pick up your younger sibling while you are in the car, they are a constant presence. I felt indirectly close to my second mami tía. I was not being informed about her life directly. I was not a part of their crew. I was a passive observer gathering the bits and pieces I overheard and feeling a sense of knowing about her life and family. And I understood she knew my life also because of how freely my mami shared her life with her in return. If something was happening, she was with my mami or my mami was with her.

It is finding familia among friends where blood ties
are formed through suffering and celebration shared.
The strength of our families never came from dom-
ination. It has only endured in spite of it—like our
women.

—Cherríe Moraga

To the husbands or romantic partners spectating a female friendship that feels threatening if only for the fact that your wife has a confidant who may peek behind the curtain of your relationship, do not feel threatened. And if you do feel threatened, may that make you adjust your behavior instead of punishing your wife through disconnection from her. Because that is what you will cause when you stand in the way of her female friendships. If isolating your wife is the only way you feel your relationship is protected, then I hope your relationship ends swiftly.

To the second mom tía, I hope that you realize how vital your existence is because your friendship with another woman teaches the girls in your life that friendships are life-giving. You teach us through these moments that we, too, might need resuscitation that only a female friendship can give. You teach us to find secondary opinions, and you teach us ways to deposit anger that we are often socialized not to express. Female friendships will save many women—you teach us that.

Through my mami's friendships, I have seen parts of her that felt surreptitious. I carry the memories of those glimpses because I cannot fulfill the role of a best friend in her life. But those moments sustain me, as a woman and now a wife. I can only hope for more of those moments for a woman I love dearly. Female friendships give us access to more of ourselves, and the gift of witnessing all that cannot be underestimated.

17

WHATSAPP TÍA

A mobile phone is the major networking tool for intra-family communication. It has surpassed, in some cases replaced, the traditional landline.

—Shriram Venkatraman

Many latinxs in the USA prefer whatsapp because that is how we stay in touch with our families back in the motherlands. Though it isn't as common in the US, WhatsApp has become a source of contact for many immigrants, and some of us have taken to the application better than others. The WhatsApp tía is one of those people who has regarded the app with care.

The WhatsApp tía is a strong archetype because it is one that exists in all our families. Depending on our levels of connection, the WhatsApp tía may be a drop in the bucket of everyone who is on WhatsApp, or she may be the sole reason you have a WhatsApp account. Her WhatsApp is always open, or it seems that way. She is often heard asking someone, "¿Tienes WhatsApp?" My WhatsApp tía is actually more of a Facebook Messenger tía, but the model remains the same.

The WhatsApp tía symbolizes yet another archetype chiseled out of displacement and trauma. My WhatsApp tía only conjures nice memories because she insists on remembering me when the alternative is to be forgotten.

War-torn countries, countries in distress, and countries whose politics have not been able to be defined by their own people but by US interventions often end up with splintered families. Families who once lived in a single block in a particular neighborhood are now all scattered throughout Latin America and the USA. When wars become the lay of the land, people who can move will move. My family is splintered. We all ended up in different countries, trying to stay connected when everything is designed to disconnect us. As of today, I have family in Panamá, México, Costa Rica, El Salvador, and various states around the USA. In the USA, we are in Georgia, Washington, DC, Tennessee, California, and Florida.

No one leaves home unless home is the mouth of a shark...You only leave home when home won't let you stay.

—Warsan Shire

I think when everyone migrates here, the expectation is that we will see one another more regularly than when we were countries apart. I remember that when my prima moved here, she had all these ideas about various excursions and road trips we would take to visit everyone who lived here. And then she was confronted with the cost of living in this country.

We are not able to afford the luxury of vacationing together or hosting family reunions. To be able to do that, to see one another regularly or even semiregularly, would mean living in an alternate universe where we would all have steady jobs with paid time off and flexibility. It takes a few generations to get that level of comfort, and for many, that level is never achieved. Most of my family works low-wage jobs or gig jobs, and consistency is far from our purview. Not only that, but not working means not earning, and so they all work; they work themselves to the bone. So instead of the ideal scenario of traveling to see one another several times a year, we stay connected through social media. Now that social media is available to most people with access to computer cafés, libraries, smartphones, and other devices, we all exist online in one way or another. Everyone in my family has Facebook, the millennials are all on Instagram, and a few are even on TikTok. And we all have WhatsApp.

Migration means that we have to push past what is in front of us and attempt to remain in the lives of loved ones we may not get to see for decades. Migration statuses will keep us away from one another, and so in some ways, that impetus to stay connected may be driven by that nation-state suppression. That need to remain tethered to people who remind you of your home country is almost a type of resistance.

The WhatsApp tía is a community organizer we seldom take the time to value and protect. Especially if we understand family as a type of community, she is someone who manages to remain available, even if just within the confines of blood relations. She puts effort into mobilizing us toward

connection with one another. She asks, she prods, she is
determined.

> *The use of Facebook and WhatsApp as communica-*
> *tive platforms between siblings happened more often in*
> *cases of sisters or sister-brother relationships than it did*
> *between brothers.*
>
> —Shriram Venkatraman

The WhatsApp tía is relentless. She will not overpour, but
she will remain a steady trickle. She sends me these gifs with
quotes and animated glitter. Sometimes she does not say much
for weeks, just gifs and quotes. Through these quotes, she tells
me I am beautiful. Through these random images she finds
on what I can only assume to be her specific algorithmic side
of the internet since I have never encountered these gifs on
my side of the World Wide Web. But she is a well of gifs and
proverbs meant to uplift. She really loves Bible quotes, often
sending me cherry-picked Bible verses meant to motivate. She
is guiding me as a tía would if you had her in person and next
to you at the dining room table. She is reminding me that her
skill sets are in communication and unification. She is virtually attempting to recreate the cocina of our abuelita's home,
hoping I will respond and give her a bit of myself that she can
latch on to. She is attempting to minister to me, like a pastor with their congregation, without overwhelming me. She is
strategically positioning herself as a beacon in my life, ensuring I know she will be around if I ever need her.

But like I said, she does not overpour. She does not message too many times without receiving some sort of sign of life. You have to give to receive, and she will give more than she receives, but she expects to receive. She wants the connection to be reciprocated, even if not with the same enthusiasm. She wants to keep the connection alive, even if it's weak on your end.

Another thing she does is send me pictures of food, specifically Nicaraguan food I grew up eating. And for a while, I was not sure if she knew that I still ate that food in the US. For a while I did not understand what her intentions were with sending me pictures of green mangoes, peeled and cut, with clumpy sea salt sprinkled on top, a Nicaraguan street food staple and one of my favorite snacks growing up. She seldom provided context for me to figure it all out. In fact, she would sometimes just click share on another Facebook post and send it to me in Messenger. And because I perceived this as impersonal, I would simply like it but not even reply. For years I did this. I was stumped.

Then it occurred to me to ask her what her posts were meant to be. I asked why she had just proceeded to send me a picture of tostones with queso frito. And she said, "Porque me recuerdo que te gustaban!" It was simple. These were things I associated with my own childhood, but they are also things she associated with my childhood. I went up and scrolled through the years of messages and realized something profound. With each image she sent me, I could attach memories directly to her.

She sent me pictures of colorful, long, and narrow popsicle sticks that are typically eaten by pushing up the popsicle through an opening at the top. I was known as Profesora Bolillo because I loved those popsicles growing up. She sent me a picture of tostones with individual cheese pieces on top of each tostón. One time, I was visiting Nicaragua alone for spring break, and she made me tostones with queso frito just like that image. And every single image I had been sent for a decade sparked a memory with her. This was and is her attempt at staying in my life by keeping our memories together alive. This is how this tía ensured I remembered that we are of the same people. This is how this tía stayed welded to me. This is how she ensured I remembered our bond.

The WhatsApp tía is like that; she will drop gems. She will not poke too much. She will not push herself onto you, that's what mamis are for. Instead, she will attempt to be nearby even if that nearby is a virtual space. She waters you, keeps you in her thoughts and prayers, and remembers you, but she gives you the space you need while trying to navigate spaces that try to remind you of your status as a foreigner. To her, you are kin, and sometimes that reminder lands perfectly. Sometimes that reminder that you *belong* somewhere is powerful enough to keep going.

Migration then becomes so embedded in certain communities that it becomes difficult to avoid as an option or as a solution to economic hardships.

—Lilia Soto

She will exist. She will have a full life wherever she is, a busy life even. But then when you pop into her head, she will reach out and send you a bendición, a prayer, words of affirmation, and maybe even a picture of a meal you have had a million times but that she remembers you shared with her. She is not sitting next to her phone waiting for you to make yourself available, that is not what she is doing; her function is so much more comprehensive than that, whether she knows it consciously or not.

The WhatsApp tía is attempting to reach beyond country lines and stay in your life. The WhatsApp tía is trying, and her efforts will be felt when they are no longer present. The WhatsApp tía is a treasure, or rather, she carries treasured memories of your life with her, and she will share those treasures with you as often as she is able. She is like a rope, waiting for when you are in need of her assistance, when the world feels hard and the obstacles are plentiful. She is waiting.

The WhatsApp tía reminds us that borders are imaginary, and family can be forever. It takes a minuscule amount of effort to keep those bonds from breaking. Migration and displacement do a lot to pull at those strings of connection, but effort is free and can work like oil on those cords and keep them lubricated enough to remain, even when they are stretched thin enough to seem invisible.

While citizenship status can be a huge reason we lose touch with our motherlands and our people, we do a bit of that all on our own too. Or better phrased, we live and work and attend institutions that encourage assimilation through dress codes, preferred dialects, socializing through different types of humor, and accepting a different lifestyle cadence. I have seen that first-generation immigrants struggle less to remain in contact, and some may even work harder to stay connected. My mom chats with her sisters regularly. She has a routine every day of sitting on her computer and chatting with them, catching up on all the illnesses, the drama with their brothers, the fights her sisters have with one another. To her, there is no question about her commitment to staying on WhatsApp to remain in contact with her kin. Back before when social media made it all easier, she would write to them often. She relied on snail mail and encomiendas sent through private local community-run services to stay in communication with her family. She was also a big international calling card lady, ensuring she would speak to her family often.

Assimilation theory predicts the steady loss of ethnic identification with time since immigration, a process that often continues into the second generation and, in a common version of that theory, is completed by the third generation.
                                    —Edward Eric Telles and Vilma Ortiz

Yet the further generations seem less interested in all that effort put into staying connected to our families in the motherlands and beyond. I fall more in the latter category since even though I was born in Nicaragua, I migrated at a really young age. My friends have become family when family was not around. I have chosen tías, older women in academia who ride hard for me and send me support online and hugs in person. I have created a substantive community here—a community that reflects my own state of being a displaced person. And having migrated here so young means that these people feel more like kin to me than my own. I have spent more years sharing myself to my chosen family than I have with my actual family. In some ways, I just want to stay with my chosen family and wish my family the best.

There are some days when I blame myself entirely for our disconnection. In this day and age there is no excuse for my lack of connection with my cousins. I tell myself it is all my fault even when phones work both ways. I carry the burden. I was very close to two particular cousins, but I've lost touch as we have all gotten married and started our own complicated lives. In some significant ways, I wonder what we would have in common now; they share different values than I do. They reflect our teachings, our very Christian beliefs around women, feminism, men's "place," gender, and sexuality. I think and live very differently than my family, and I wonder if we can even still be anything to one another. We feel estranged.

I do not perceive them as discardable. In fact, maybe I should risk it all and attempt to have difficult conversations with them, even when I am tired of having those conversations with everyone I grew up alongside.

But they are my connection to my roots in more ways than I can name. While I have a lot of friendships with Latin American people, and even a lot of Central Americans, being Nicaraguan is still core to my identity. And in community with Nicaraguans, I find myself so at ease. I deeply understand our humor, our posture, our customs, and our foods.

Because of that, I am now trying to crawl back to those links to my heritage, and I'm finding dried-up wells from my own lack of involvement. I find myself even adapting some of the WhatsApp tía's skills in my own pursuit of connection with my family back home. And that is my own bridge to build, on my own terms, and hopefully for the sake of finding more opportunities to have symbiotic exchanges around ideas and worldviews.

To the family of the WhatsApp tía, it has been documented that it is women who do this type of labor. So I also want to encourage y'all to raise boys to become men who also feel obligated to perform this type of crucial emotional work for their own families. This work is not only female labor; nothing is an exclusively female thing. It should not be expected of the women in the family to carry out this task. In fact, I would encourage more fathers to become beacons of connectivity to set an example of what it means to try to remain connected. I still know my mother's side of the family like they live next door to me through the ways my mom and her sisters have stayed consistent in one another's lives. And yet, I know little of my father's side of the family because my father and his brothers do not make that concerted daily effort. In a family of men, they speak when things are bad or when someone is dying, but they seldom communicate about the good and the mundane. I want to encourage more men to seek out true connection to their families, lest we lose y'all entirely.

To the WhatsApp tía, I hope you realize that you are a critical element to our family units. Regardless of the range of responses you receive, know that you are doing significant emotional labor to protect something you believe to be sacred: family. I want to encourage you to continue to do what you are doing, but you do not need me to remind you of that. What I do want to encourage you to think about is how much different the children of your siblings may be from how you remember them. I want to encourage you to see what they are trying to show you through their social media posts and responses. Being seen is a powerful thing, and there is no greater feeling than feeling seen by your own family, even thousands of miles away.

18

LA TÍA CUIR

Familial concerns regarding femininity deployment are intertwined and cannot be extracted from the reservations those families of origin had regarding their children's alternative sexualities.

—Katie L. Acosta

I HAVE THIS TÍA WHO I HAVE LOST, BUT SHE IS STILL ALIVE. SHE IS NOT A biological tía. She grew up with my mami's family and lived in the house next to my abuelita's the entire time I knew her. I believe her mami still lives there today. She was reliably always there, peeking through a small opening in her rose garden that she created for ease of access to the chest-high gate that separated our houses' front porches. I grew up with her just as much as I grew up with my own biological tías. Because I understand that family is not just blood, to me, she is just as important and just as invaluable, although mi mami probably resented the association. And while I could play with her and hang out with her through the fence, I was forbidden from going into her home.

Not only was I not allowed to go to her home—which again was right next door to my abuelita's, close enough that you could hear any conversation happening next door just by standing on mi abuelita's front porch—she was rarely invited or allowed into my grandmother's house. I did not know this growing up, but I learned about it years later. This tía, this very important person in my young life, was not welcomed inside my family's home, and I innocently defied everyone by loving her regardless. Or maybe I was not so innocent about it. I always sensed there was something no one was telling me, and I ran with the fear they had about "protecting my innocence" by not uttering the truth. My favorite tía is cuir.

Your tía cuir is someone who you may not have always understood to be cuir, as she may have come out later in life. Or you may have grown up with her being an out cuir person. My tía cuir was not out. So I now see our experiences as cuir-coded, but only in hindsight. I now see the rejection I witnessed being directed toward her by the straight women in my household as highly homophobic.

Growing up, she did not automatically dress like other women in my family did, adhering to gender norms and respectability politics. As a kid, all the other women in my life wore dresses or skirts, and when wearing shorts, you had to have a pastel top or something that signaled your gender, and she did not. Mi mami wore long pastel dresses; it was the '80s and early '90s, and that was the fashion of that era. I wore dresses regularly myself; that is how I was dressed. This tía looked comfiest in a baggy white T-shirt and shorts, and she kept her hair undone. Unlike the women in my family, she did not put on a dress. I think she knew she stood out, this difference was obvious, because that is how femininity was inscribed in our community and in my abuelita's particular working-class neighborhood, Bello Horizonte. Her white T-shirts and denim or cargo shorts stood in stark contrast.

> *This process is more complicated than simply choosing a more professional appearance in the workplace versus a relaxed look for the weekends. Situational femininities are meticulously planned and involve an array of physical appearances. Doing situational femininities requires the actor to consider her audience and the expectations for gender performance within this specific space and produce that specific version of femininity in order to gain access.*
> —Katie L. Acosta

She rarely wore a bra when she was home—who does? And when I saw her, she was at home. I should also mention that this is not a detail I remember. This is a detail imprinted onto me by mi mami, who seemed very committed to dissuading me from interacting with this tía I loved so much. I would have never noticed on my own, but the other women in my family would talk about her every time they got the chance—and always behind her back. As a girl, I grew up in close proximity to the chatter of women; I grew up hearing them speak, though rarely to me and often in hushed tones so only those around them could hear.

I think I made everyone uncomfortable with how much I wanted her around. At the occasional times when she came inside my grandmother's home, it was thanks to an uncle who liked talking to her; whenever he visited, she got an invitation. He was around her age, and they had gone to school together when they were kids. They were friends, or at least friendly. I loved seeing her, and I would sit by her, sensing how much everyone else wanted her gone. It was so obvious in their lack of effort to connect with her, how she would quickly find her way outside, the briefness of it all. I knew it was unpleasant for everyone involved. But I never knew why, or rather, their reasons behind how they acted never made sense. Her queerness today feels so clear.

Mi tía cuir was always watching me, taking care of me, but not too closely like an overbearing parent. She had all boys from a previous marriage, and they watched me too. They took care of me; they kept an eye on me no matter where I was. They were the kind big brothers I never had, and I was the little sister they never had. They were tasked with taking care of me, and we all knew it. They were often nicer to me than my own brother.

Mi tía cuir would stand back, smiling and never smothering. She watched, her back to the wall with one leg up, smoking her cigarettes and watching intently to make sure I was staying off the street while I played.

When I lived in Nicaragua, every birthday I would have a separate celebration just with this tía. She would make my favorite dish, gallo pinto con Coca-Cola. She would also have cake for me, queque con leche condensada. And we would celebrate my birthday just me, her, and her son who was my age. We would set up a table on the sidewalk in front of mi abuelita's home to abide by the rules of engagement. Her son was one of my best friends, and he always treated me so well because his mami told him that was how women should be treated. I do not have many memories of Nicaragua that do not include her and her son. They were crucial to me and my development. This tía felt very similar to my young tía (who was now a mami herself and has engaged in this distancing from this tía along with her sisters). She saw me, and I felt seen by her.

Mi tía cuir spoke to me like I mattered, and nothing I did was annoying to her but was merely a by-product of my age. She had the softest center that no other adult seemed to want to display. Mi tía cuir always made time. It always felt like all her time was for me. She cleared her days when I would visit every Sunday, and then when we migrated and would come from the US to visit, she would clear her weeks.

When we migrated, she was one of the few adults who cried about not seeing me again. Our migration felt rushed and hard to wrap my mind around—I was only seven years old—but I remember her crying and wiping her tears with her white over-size T-shirt. Her tears were for me, and I knew that. I knew we had a special bond. We were close. I remember her good-bye; it is one of my only memories of that experience. I don't even remember my own biological tías' reactions to us leaving, but I remember this tía's reaction. She mourned my departure; I felt special to her, and she felt special to me.

Mi tía cuir taught me to be soft, and she taught me to be kind. Through her, I learned at a very early age that sometimes adults are mean because I saw how cruel my family was behind her back. I heard it all, and I felt protective of her. I felt like they were talking about a good friend of mine, but I also knew better than to say anything. We both protected our access to each other; it was precious. She played by their rules, and I played by their rules too. In some significant ways, we were both powerless. She was powerless because she was not biologically related to me, and I was powerless because I was a little girl.

It was most obvious when we all went outdoors how little regard my family had for her, especially the women in my family. In the evenings, everyone in my family home will get on rocking chairs and sit in the front porch area. It is a routine, a ritual we perform. The nights are cooler, none of our family homes have air conditioning, and it is the perfect time to open all the windows and doors. It is the time to bring all the mecedoras outside and put your feet up. This is when the family interacts with this aunt since she is relegated to being outdoors. However, while she was always eager to see me, she seldom appeared as eager to be with the other adults.

I would hear many stories from the women in my family as attempts to smear her shine in my eyes. The eye rolls, the whispers, the snickering—it was so painfully obvious on our faces. While she was not out, her unwillingness to act like a "proper" woman, her lack of shame for being an unwed woman, and her queer-coded, gender-bending posturing made the women hate her. This tía's in-betweenness seemed to upset them, and they did not care to hide their disdain. She smoked, she cursed, she spoke to men without an inch of respect, and her posture was so straight around them that it even bent backward a bit as she puffed her chest in confidence. She did not perform for men, and I think that felt threatening.

*Lesbians unsettle the basis of both hegemonic mascu-
linity and heteronormativity by rejecting compulsory
heterosexuality.*

—Justin Charlebois

This tía leaves tough conversations to go smoke whenever
she is fed up with adults. That after-dinner rocking chair ritual is when everyone chats. She is seldom invited to sit in a
rocking chair with us, so she stands on her side of the fence
and chats, mostly with the children or the men. Sometimes I
think this tía reflects the parts of us that we want to reject,
but they reflect us and are a part of us no matter how much
distance has come between.

At some point, I stopped seeing this tía altogether. I was
eventually told that she was living with another woman. The
way my mom spoke that into the room—only after I asked, as
if I needed no explanation for her absence unless I asked for
her—made my skin crawl. My mom still rejected her even in
her absence.

The sheen of admiration I had for my parents began to
erode the more aware I became of how much they rejected my
tía cuir, whom I loved so much. I will always resent everyone
in my family for how they treated her, for thinking that the
children were too dumb to pick up on the nuances. I always
knew; I just knew not to defend her because it would risk my
access to her. I knew to tread lightly. They gave me that wonderful trauma response of reading a room and finding tools for
surviving in what was not said, but implied. I still feel a need
to read people's body language and to expect a policing based

on unsaid biases. I don't enter rooms with excitement; I enter rooms and start plotting ways to survive them.

Because queerness was criminalized in my country until very recently, she went into hiding, and I do not ask further questions of my family. In fact, I have grown to have such a distaste for any type of rejection of her that I won't even ask her one son I still see around about her. He has become my family's favorite of her sons because he is Christian and has a wife and kids. He is doing what men are expected to do; he is doing his gender-specific role. Due to his obedience, he can be spoken to with respect. To them, he is a reflection of good character and not of her parenting. My mind, therefore, has made him one of them, and I cannot seem to convince myself that he is someone who will hold space for my desire to connect with her today even when I know nothing of their relationship.

Their hatred for her feels so personal now, and their rejection of her makes me so angry. I know if I want to find her, I will have to do it myself, and I intend on doing that next time I visit my country alone.

Everyone I have asked seems not to know where she lives anymore, and no one seems to know how to contact her. It is like they preferred her cuirness to exist without evidence. I will always begrudge my family for placing conditions on how we accepted her, but then I remember that we all lived under conditions, and that is probably sadder for them. Who knows how much they have kept inside themselves out of fear of rejection, a rejection they brandished so freely. Ultimately, she was a threat to everyone else.

Looking back at my own history, achieving dominant
femininity was a way for female kin to bond.
                                        —Katie L. Acosta

Today, I am very distant from a lot of my own family for
a lot of reasons, but I will always remember their conditional
love. Instead, I have a hoard of chosen family, a strong group
of lesbian, queer, and trans women who love me deeper than
anyone blood-related ever has because we have all felt the sting
of conditional love and dare to never love with such fickleness
again.

I have seen my cuir friends come out to their families and
receive wrath instead of acceptance. I have held my friends
while they have cried because their kin no longer wanted anything to do with them. I have been in group texts with a friend
going through the ups and downs of navigating their cuirness
around a family who prefers they do not bring it up. I have kept
my own coming-out away from the grasp of my parents, who
will predictably react in the same ways my friends' parents have
because I got a front-row seat to how they spoke about a cuir
person my entire life. I know exactly how they feel. I do not
give them access to hurt that part of me. I refuse to let them
hurt that part of me, the part of me that is not negotiable.

I have no way of knowing how to reach this tía, but I want
her to know that I love her and that she deserves to live a life
full of love. She is worthy of receiving the same love that she
gave me growing up. She is not only worthy and deserving in
the ways that we all are, but in the way that when life throws

you stones and you manage to dodge them all, what is waiting for you after that downpour had better fucking be strictly sunshine. I hope her partner is kind and tender. I hope her partner is el sol because she was mine.

I have this tía who is cuir, and she has been shunned for it, and all I wish is to tell her that I am cuir too. I am protective of her because she taught me to be protective of myself and my own magic. I have never felt shame toward her because she was the one who taught me that being cuir makes you softer toward those you love and those who love you back.

I have this tía whom I might never see again, but I hope that she is happy, wherever she is. I hope that she is safe. To the tía who is cuir, rejection is probably a feeling you may be all too familiar with, but I hope that when you receive acceptance, you receive it tenfold. I wish I had known you as an adult; I would have known how to protect you. I would have known how to stand up for us. To the tía who is cuir, your silence is your safety, and through you I learned that not everyone needs access to hurt us. I learned to guard myself against those who have rejected you because if they knew I am cuir, they would reject me too.

For the tías who snickered, rolled their eyes, and showed disdain for the queer tía, figure out what that hatred is rooted in and find compassion for yourself. Whoever taught you that love is conditional—that is who deserves your disdain, not the person living her life and loving whomever she wants to love. The lesson here is to mothers who find themselves sharing family spaces with cuir folks and find it in themselves to utilize that person's queerness as a child-rearing tool cloaked with homophobia: do not do this. You are harming your child, and you are only creating more obstacles for them to feel unconditionally loved by you. You are creating conditions right before their very eyes. Do better by everyone in the room and dare to show compassion instead.

A woman is all the more respected if she "presents well"; the more she needs to find work, the more useful it is to look well-off: elegance is a weapon, a sign, a banner of respect, a letter of recommendation.

—Simone de Beauvoir

My cuir tía showed me compassion all the time, and what my parents managed to show her was disrespect when they should have been grateful for how much she loved their daughter. My cuir friends who are tías are the best people I know. I think when you see rejection so intimately you grow cautious of throwing people away, and I have grown cautious of throwing people away. While some cuir family members may be allowed into their family gatherings, there is always that tía who leaves and gets in her car with her family and spews homophobia, ensuring her children become afraid of ever coming out to her.

I want my tía cuir to know that I am grateful for her. Thank you for teaching me those invaluable lessons. You deserved the world, and yet what you received was a small opening in the rosebush on your fence, which you created. A metaphor for your insistence to be seen, a light among darkness, the mightiest rose in your garden.

19

MLM TÍA

Predatory companies also target recent-immigrant communities, minority communities, and lower-income communities worldwide. Many of these groups are known for valuing family and community, are upwardly mobile, and have close, trusting connections. A single foothold in a tight-knit community is valuable for recruitment because communities that value cohesion are likely to produce more recruits or, at the very least, more buyers.

—Mona Bushnell

I HAVE SEEN MULTI-LEVEL MARKETING (MLM) SCHEMES WREAK HAVOC IN my own family and my own community of immigrants. The way I have seen MLMs take over a household is that it all starts out very exciting. Emotionally, it is the feeling of fresh hope. There is this lie that MLMs hold over those they prey upon, and that is that they will change your life. If you play your cards right, you too can reach the American dream. You too will reach class mobility. You too can have access to the

illusive notion of success America says it offers. Emotionally,
MLMs feel like a promise. A promise that things will change
and that long-term generational financial struggles can finally
end. But in reality, success in these models seldom comes to
fruition.

I have seen Mary Kay women in our church subsist on a
few loyal fellow church women buying their products exclusively from them. These women were doing it to supplement
their income, working their trade or manual labor jobs and
adding a few bucks to their wallets along the way. No one did
this as their only source of money. And yet seldom did these
women blame the company models. They blamed themselves
for their inability to gain more loyal customers.

I was very young when my dad got caught up in Amway.
I remember this one charismatic church leader who was
traveling across our local church plants chatting up the dads.
I remember my mom talking about it with displeasure in
her tone. Once she figured out what was happening, as per
usual, decisions had already been made without her input,
and we were an Amway family. My dad saw this wealthy man
selling these products, and this promise of a payout, and he
thought it must have been Amway that led to his success, not
his already well-established wealth. This man was just getting
richer.

In the beginning, it also feels possible. Soon there are
boxes full of goodies at your front door, and you cannot help
but think how luxurious the products all look and feel. It gives
the illusion of abundance, even if those are products that rely

on your ability to sell them. The boxes feel like a Christmas morning.

The next thing I knew there were these boxes sitting on our dining room table for months because my dad could not sell a single thing since the church member who sold my dad on Amway also sold everyone else in our church on it. This man was traveling to all the church plants, filled with new immigrants, across the United States. It would soon become a topic of conversation and stay one for as long as those products sat on our dining room table untouched. Our only real community members that he could have sold these products to were all dealing with having no buyers of their own, and we were all staring at these boxes wondering if we should just use the products ourselves so they wouldn't go to waste.

Becoming a direct seller requires no previous experience, no formal education, and little startup capital, so it is particularly attractive when other forms of employment are scarce.

—Peter S. Cahn

No one I knew had a pink Mary Kay car, which is touted as the goal. Yet at some point that goal turns into a pipe dream, a unicorn that will incite squeals when you finally lay your eyes on the one pink Mary Kay car driving on the road. I saw my pink Mary Kay car once in an upper-middle-class suburban neighborhood in Miami that one of my middle school friends lived in. I had to do a double take because I was not sure I could believe my eyes. That once-in-a-lifetime apparition.

Most recently, I saw MONAT haircare take over my undergrad sorority, which was full of Latinas. One by one, I got the emails from alumni who were all selling MONAT. And you have these moments when you feel simultaneously bad for them, and then annoyed that you are receiving these sales emails disguised as genuine connections. But then I remember that the cost of living continues to increase while we have barely raised the minimum wage. Not to mention the wage gap between genders and races, so non-Black Latinas and Black women continue trying to stay afloat, and there are plenty of reasons to join MLMs. Miami has gone from an immigrant-friendly city to something unrecognizably expensive, and many of my old friends have to move into their families' home additions or leave the city to find cheaper living options. The promise of some extra money, even if that takes over your days off, still offers a better alternative over nothing. And soon, those emails from alumni start to feel significantly more and more reasonable, even when I understand that the large machine hovering over this entire scheme is profiting off the shitty situations of others.

Many choose to leave the business, but they are replaced by others who seek a self-help solution to their financial problems.

—Peter S. Cahn

Herbalife took over my church after I stopped attending. I heard it through the grapevine. Churches seem to be prime locations for these schemes to take off. This particular line of products promised consistent customers because it demanded constant consumption. The señoras who love dieting were quick to become the first to start buying and then selling the products. And pretty soon, everyone was drinking Herbalife and trying to figure out how to sell it to others. Immigrants and women seem to increasingly get caught in these schemes, and so this archetype felt important for a book on Latina archetypes. These corporations profit by exploiting the thing we all need to live: more money.

The fact is that MLM schemes run rampant in communities that are close-knit. Because Latines often find themselves in such communities out of necessity, they are consistently quick to get wrapped up in these schemes. MLMs make promises of flexible work schedules and endless piles of money, and all of that strikes a chord with specific communities. MLMs are often just shiny hooks with bait on them, and in the end, those promises do not turn into anything much more than added work to already busy lives with little to no benefit. And many people leave these MLMs quietly and feeling ashamed.

The truth of the matter is that the American dream is often an American terror. Many new immigrants think that coming to this country means immediate success because of what television shows them about its white citizens. You must have the deck stacked in your favor to get to live the life often depicted on television, meaning if you are migrating to the USA with family wealth, you are preferably white or white-passing and have other family already here who are ready to help in any way they can and have secured long-term employment that is paying you a living wage—then you are set. But in actuality, if you migrate to the USA, you usually come here to work, and you work till you cannot work anymore. The cycle of being overworked for little pay is life-sucking. You may put your hopes on the later generations, hoping they will have it easier through adapting to the language and culture, yet they probably will attend underfunded schools being taught by outsiders with internalized biases. You are already at a deficit for struggling, and working hard will not lead you out of that struggle.

> *Class is a potent force in health and longevity in the United States. The more education and income people have, the less likely they are to have and die of heart disease, strokes, diabetes, and many types of cancer. Upper middle-class Americans live longer and in better health than middle-class Americans, who live longer and better than those at the bottom. And the gaps are widening.*
>
> —Janny Scott

The cycles of systemic oppression start to feel hopeless really fast. MLM schemes often find their victims primed and ready for exploitation because being victim of something you cannot see but know is there feels alarming. But becoming pawns for something tangible at least gives us something to blame; the real monster is capitalism.

Meritocracy is pushed like propaganda. I was consistently told that hard work is all it takes to be successful, and whenever someone was struggling, it was always explicitly or implicitly said that it was because they were lazy. Yet what we see every day is hardworking people staying one or two paychecks away from homelessness. The truth of the matter is that one medical emergency, one vehicular malfunction, or even one family death can leave a lot of working-class people struggling to pay their bills. And most painfully of all, we blame ourselves for these circumstances.

Meritocracy stays blaming us for our circumstances. It is difficult to accept that the American dream is a lie. It is easier to keep trying other avenues. To accept that you have moved to a new country with seemingly less dangerous politics, yet you find that what it has promised is actually not what it is giving you. It is moving you into a position of victimhood. And no one wants to be a victim; nobody wants to accept that they are smaller and less powerful than their circumstances. We all want to believe we are capable of anything. We have to believe we are capable of anything.

The American Myth also provides a means of laying blame. In the Puritan legacy, hard work is not merely practical but also moral; its absence suggests an ethical lapse. A harsh logic dictates a hard judgement: If a person's diligent work leads to prosperity, if work is a moral virtue, and if anyone in the society can attain prosperity through work, then the failure to do so is a fall from righteousness.

—David K. Shipler

Surely, this new MLM will be different.

Surely, the assurance of the pursuit of happiness has to mean something.

But the truth of the matter is that your MLM tía has got a lot of grit. She dares to keep pushing. She commits to selling a product she believes in, which is better than selling a product you do not believe in. I have found myself resenting MLM tías and primas in my life because I want better for them, but what I have discovered is that they want better for themselves too. We have a common goal, and to resent their strategies for that goal and not the systems that put them in those positions is a fault on my end.

To the family of the MLM tía, I want to encourage y'all and acknowledge the position you are all in. It will be clear as day to understand what has made this tía particularly vulnerable to these schemes if you lead with critical thinking skills. I want us to help guide this tía away from these community-exploiting schemes and more toward sustainable living through community-based relationships. Being preyed upon sucks; having to find other means of supplementing one's income sucks; the lack of a living wage across this country sucks.

To the MLM tía, you have done nothing wrong in trying to find a new outlet to reach a dream that feels unreachable.

But truthfully, these MLMs can erode friendships. When the products do not work, as many do not, you have to contend with the clientele, who are often people in your community. The payoff never compensates for the loss that is experienced when people realize they have been swindled. I want to encourage you not to blame yourself, but also look closely at what you are participating in. Sometimes in our resolve to get out of a bind, we can become individualistic, and individualism will not save us. We will save one another.

20

YOUR "PRETTY" PRIMA

The disciplinary power that inscribes femininity in the female body is everywhere and it is nowhere; the disciplinarian is everyone and yet no one in particular.

—Sandra Lee Bartky

I DO NOT THINK EVERY LATIN AMERICAN FAMILY HAS THIS ARCHETYPE TO the extreme that I will present it, but I have seen this archetype with enough regularity to include it in this book. I have also never seen this written about whatsoever. But the "pretty" prima is an unavoidable reality in many working-class people of color spaces, which is the context I am most familiar with due to my own upbringing. This is not an invisible archetype, but maybe we have not had the language to name the particular circumstances around this prima's reality. This archetype is hypervisible, yet so normalized that I think we have accepted her as fact and do not challenge it all enough.

The first time I saw the pretty prima, in all her glory, was at a Christian conference. I attended and was raised in a very conservative Latine Christian tradition. A few times a year we had youth conferences, another conference for pastors and their families, and even a national conference where all the North American families of all the church plants across the USA and Canada were invited to attend. For context, my church tradition, while Latine, was also mostly non-Black.

At these conferences, I met this pretty prima. Her dad was one of the pastors in one of the church plants in North America.

When the pretty prima walked into a room, she looked like any other girl to me. She was pretty, but I had not fully accepted European standards of beauty into my psyche at the time when I met her in my early teens. I am far from European-looking, and it would take a few more years for me to fully hate myself in relation to what I was watching unfold before me. In this era, I was starting to become acutely aware of it all, but it was not my full position yet.

While she did possess European features, she was brown, mestiza, with dark, wavy hair. It was in her facial features where you saw those things we associate with whiteness: her nose was small, her ears were tiny, her wrists were small, and her waist was small. She was fifteen or sixteen when I first met her. And I should note that out of her sisters, she was not the lightest-skinned one in her family, but she performed a more traditional femininity. That is the thing about colorism as it applies to women—it colludes with femininity. This is all about looking and absorbing European ideals of beauty through a close-enough-to-whiteness presentation. All the things we are told that women should be, she appeared to possess. She was a girl with what we would traditionally think of as having "womanlike" features.

> *Unlike boys, whose market value increases through participation in athletics and student government, girls' value is measured by and contingent upon their attractiveness, personality and social adeptness, which are feminine resources that can be used to secure heterosexual alliances.*
>
> —Justin Charlebois

What was most striking about her was the group of boys who surrounded her everywhere she went. It became sort of a joke between my friends and me. A joke we told ourselves to avoid the fact that maybe we were the joke. That maybe we were the ones who were on the losing side of this equation. It was a joke to keep us from being crushed under the weight of not being her. We were the few who were even attempting to figure out what was happening.

We could get away with hell when she entered a room because the boys flocked to her like she was a celebrity, and the parents all looked to ensure she was behaving accordingly, respectfully, even when the boys had passed the point of decorum. It was written in stone; she would someday soon have her pick of a man, and she had better pick wisely.

On any given day, when she was around, she could have ten boys surrounding her. It was cartoonish. Like when Bugs

Bunny first sees Honey Bunny, that was the pretty prima to every boy near her age. Seeing these boys lose it over a young girl was daunting.

This was overt heteronormativity, and they were okay with its expressions; it was "expected." The men could be assertive in their attraction, and the onus was on her to keep them at bay. And as long as everyone played their roles well, there was nothing to correct. This was a performance, and a suitable suitor was to see his prize coveted. But the eerie underpinning of this is that a prized girl could pick a prized man, and a prized man in very many working-class circles is often one who provides financial stability, maybe even upward mobility. The pretty prima's role is to marry well; marrying above your family's status was highly desired and encouraged. Elevating the family name and status is a game, and pretty girls are pawns.

My parents were friends with her parents, and how her parents spoke of the pretty prima's beauty was uncomfortable. We were all girls, and this prima was two years older than me, but we were girls. And the open dialogue around her physical appearance made me uncomfortable, especially when it came from her parents. To watch parents invest so much energy in glorifying the physical appearance of their daughter was in stark contrast to what I was taught at home.

The idea that you could make a man sin through his thoughts due to how you dressed or carried yourself, that was something to be mindful of in our church tradition. It is fucked up, and it is rape culture at its finest, but that was the church culture I grew up in. In my home, women were not to be ogled at physically. To be vanidosa was something to be mindful of. To be read as someone who was physically alluring as a woman was a big no-no in my home. That is not to say that this prima was doing anything to bring that attention on herself, yet this is the framing we were told to absorb within the same church traditions we were all part of, so to watch it and not have them all correlate it as that was odd. Furthermore, my brother could display interest in someone who did take care to present herself through what my context would call vain tools, including but not limited to makeup.

We were shamed for allowing others to see us across all our church plants. Meanwhile, her parents seemed to exalt it, welcome the praises, and even show pride in how many people admired their daughter. I have sat for many years contemplating why this happened, and why it was also so unspoken, to critically attempt to make sense of it, and ultimately my conclusion is European standards of beauty, traditional femininity, and heteronormativity are used as social capital.

In aspiring to femininity girls are encouraged to seek power through their appearance and their manners. The ideal of femininity is pretty, nice, desirable, and popular. Truth be told, there is real power in this ideal but it is borrowed power, granted power.

—Sharon Lamb

To be considered desirable and have smaller European facial features is also to attain proximity to whatever whiteness has taught us is beautiful. I imagine it as close to white privilege, though not quite. But it means having the world opened up to you differently than it would for someone darker, bigger, or with a wider nose, etc. We like to refer to this type of beauty as "universally good-looking," but what we should really call it is white or undeniably close enough to whiteness. For many non-Black Latin Americans, whiteness is the goal, so much so that we have terms like blanqueamiento and phrases like "mejorar la raza" as references within our culture. We are really caught up in whiteness and how to get access to it if at all possible. Whiteness or proximity to whiteness is supported by the systems in place, and even today lightness means power.

I have started asking Latin American women if they had a pretty sister, cousin, or aunt, and I also ask if they were treated differently than them. Some of the women I asked looked at me like I was crazy to even be focused on a woman's appearance. But sometimes there is this moment of *aha!* that occurs when I ask that same question to someone who deeply understands this because they have experienced it personally.

I had one woman tell me that her pretty sister was sent to private school while the rest of the siblings were sent to public school. I had someone tell me that they were the pretty sister, and they noticed a huge difference between their treatment and that of their other sisters. Grandparents had even given them nicknames to match their preferred status. One said she was taken out shopping regularly, often upgrading her wardrobe to her growing body while the siblings were not. The pretty cousin is constantly reminded that she is pretty and gets doted on by adults with perverted admiration. The memories of having seen this preferential treatment of one child over the others are hard to shake, but also, I think our brains want to rid themselves of ugly truths like this one.

The pretty prima represents a caste system that we seldom want to openly discuss, unless we are aware of what popular advocates against colorism in Latin America have been saying. I think ultimately, the pretty prima represents a ticket out of poverty. The hyperfixation on her beauty is truthfully a hyperfixation on class mobility.

Because we all function within a race-conscious society, how we value people is directly related to the color of their skin and their features. Aspirational whiteness is the underbelly of non-Black Latin American people's value system. When we are gifted with a systemically enforced example of beauty within our own families, we see potential. And that is because when we see success in Latin America, we see whiteness. We have been taught that whiteness means wealth, success, and fame. It is so embedded that even when we should be seeing a beloved new member of our family, we see money.

When entire peoples have been told that proximity to whiteness is the key to power, watching parents exploit their young girls' European-like beauty makes sense. When we have accepted it as a fundamental truth, it does not feel like the predatory behavior that it is.

But we need to call it what it is: it is icky. Also, it is no different than the regular treatment of women in Latin America, where femicide rates are through the roof. Not to mention that many of us come from countries where even miscarriages are criminalized. Domestic abuse is still so rampant throughout, and this is all true because we do not view women as worthy of choices, respect, life. We are viewed as conquerable, capable of being dominated. This is simply another violent act performed toward women—business as usual. The ease with which we oppress women cannot be overlooked. In regard to the pretty prima, they have normalized that her value is directly related to her appearance, and then they expect her to develop into a healthy, well-rounded human being. We are all complicit when we allow that behavior to continue.

> *Beauty and ugliness became as much principles of human classification as material factors of measurements, climate, and the environment. The Racial Contract makes the white body the somatic norm, so that in early racist theories one finds not only moral but aesthetic judgments, with beautiful and fair races pitted against ugly and dark races.*
>
> —C. Wright Mills

It is hard to demonize one specific family knowing that these systems of oppression are vicious, and oppressed people have often internalized vicious strategies to outsmart oppression. Our backs have been up against a wall for centuries. And while I am all for outsmarting systems of oppression, it is survival. But at some point, we have to realize how stunting the entire charade really is. Generations within our own families can be affected through outsmarting these systems, but it is individualistic.

We have exploited the fact that we socialize girls to be sweet and kind, and then we have driven our lust for upward mobility into them. What this says about us is that we have all absorbed their fucked-up systems, and to expect to gain anything from it brings up an ethical conundrum: What about the little girl?

It can feel encouraging that this type of behavior may "save" your family tree, but you have changed nothing to prevent this from happening to more little girls. Instead, you have taken a little girl's agency for a potential gain without her consent.

The losing party in all this is the little girl. In a society that discards darker-skinned people, heaping all your hopes and dreams onto her feels unfair, at best. At worst, you have sold your daughters for power, and I don't know how you can live with that other than to think we have normalized this as a society and repackaged it for our comfort. Is blanqueamiento worth your daughters? Is wealth worth grooming little girls to marry well? Is it worth everything you gamble along the way?

What I have seen is that some of these pretty primas can become resentful of their situation. The pretty primas in working-class families have learned that their beauty is a ticket, and the minute they can exercise some of their agency as they start growing up and being left to their own devices, they will learn to wield that beauty, and not always in the ways their parents imagined. They can use what they were told to use for their betterment to avenge themselves.

What was taught to her is that beauty can get you things, and she may at some point use that information to do whatever her heart desires. A parent of a pretty prima may not have spent enough time nurturing her heart. The overemphasis on outer beauty does not mean that you taught them to be kind, anti-racist, anti-transphobic, anti-misogynistic, justice-seeking, or community-oriented. Instead, a parent of the pretty prima may have taught her that she can benefit from her outer beauty and reinforced an individualistic model in which that parent might be left out of it. And it serves them right; I hope they are left with broken promises and dreams unrealized. The pretty prima's life was never theirs to take for their aspirations, and yet they did it anyway.

If they reject their family's wishes and somehow do not place their assets in the right place and at the right time, they may not find the ticket you are looking for. They may even marry whomever they please, maybe someone from a similar if not lower economic background. I have seen pretty primas rebel—hard. I have seen them "dishonor" their families. I have seen the pretty primas fight back, but why were they put in that situation to begin with?

As a daughter who wasn't the pretty prima but was primed to be a pure prima, I took revenge hard on my parents and slept around openly to spite them. The people who are the most hurt when our value system is skewed are the girls you should have worried about parenting more instead of having them become receptacles of your unresolved trauma.

To the families at large who have these value systems deeply rooted in their psyche, relinquish these narratives so that no more girls are used as tools. To the families who have absorbed maladaptive skills around a world of conquerors and conquered, if you are resisting abandoning these awful survival skills, may you rot in hell. This prima's predicament is not seemingly bad; it may even require us to investigate pretty privilege within the context of her life. However, her lack of agency in this is what should be troubling. While a few of the archetypes are a result of internalized isms that make someone an outcast, this internalized ism puts this prima on a pedestal that may be more harmful than we realize. We need to evaluate what is within us and our worship of whiteness that results in the overvaluing of proximity to it. We need to raise daughters who believe themselves to be worthy of respect regardless of what their outward appearance may be.

For the pretty prima, I wish healing for you. You were always worthy, even when you were made to feel like your worth was specifically tied to your looks. You always mattered, and you should have been spoken to more than spoken at.

To the pretty prima, may we make penance for worshipping at the church of whiteness and femininity and all that bullshit for far too long. To the pretty prima, you owe no one a single thing, especially your family members who placed their selfish ambitions on you. To the pretty prima, you deserve the world just like any other prima in your life. I hope that you create boundaries for yourself around your family so that they begin to see the error of their ways, even from a distance. I wish for you inner peace and a life free of pretty girl expecta-tions. If you find that your contemporaries, girls in your family, may resent you, I implore everyone in these scenarios to extend more grace toward yourselves. You all have been harmed by what we have been force-fed, and we all deserved better than what we were given.

CONCLUSION

They were hard-edged, soft-centered, brutally demand-ing, and easily pleased.

—Gloria Naylor

WHEN I FIRST DREAMED OF THIS BOOK, THE ILLUSTRATIONS WERE KEY to how I wanted it to look and feel. I wanted something that felt familiar, even if just to my own context. I wanted to name real things I have seen, real issues I have normalized, things I saw that I did not fully understand but understand better today. And there were real images attached to everything I wrote down, everything I named. I do not write into the void; I do not write for the sake of writing. I write to help others feel seen. I write with particular women in mind, and those people look like the women in this book. I am all of the women in this book, in one way or another. They represent my inner fears, my deepest struggles, my best qualities, and my demons. I am the women who helped shape me, the women I admired from afar and tried to emulate, and the women who tried to shift me into becoming their wildest dreams. In writing this I felt a sense of healing and a closeness to myself and my grandmothers that transcends. Some of us grow up held literally by our abuelitas and tías and primas, and some of us had to hold them in our hearts as we navigated this world. And even as I presented the complicated women in these pages, I long for them still. I long for their teachings, I long to chat with them for hours, and I long to hear them laugh more than anything in this entire world.

What I hope is that in these pages you felt seen and that things were named for you that might've otherwise gone unnamed. In naming the forces at play in our lives, we can take back some control. By keeping us in the normalization space of "this is how it has always been done," they take our agency away. I want to give us back what should have always been available to us: the ability to push back and question and grow. In having real conversations with our kin, chosen or otherwise, we can step into a space of knowing ourselves better. In community, we can mobilize and change things, but it takes the proper tools. I hope I gave you some tools. Tools I am learning to use better with each day that passes.

I have made relics of the women in my life; I have built shrines in my homes to both of my grandmothers. I have tattooed their flowers on my body to protect their memories. I wanted to keep them with me as I transformed because something needed to stay the same even as I changed beyond what they would both call a respectable woman. It felt important to have something steady, even if just in my imagination. Changing and growing beyond our family traumas is a lonely road, especially if your family, like mine, is against the concept of therapy and thinks healing is something only God can provide. As I heal, I find myself writing about the women in my life. May it do for you whatever it needs to do.

When my grandmothers became ancestors, I tried to keep them alive within me. I have sat with memories and tried to pinpoint smells and recall what people wore during specific times. And as I prepared myself to reincarnate them from memories in this book, I started to see so much more than I had seen before. I realized how much I truly do miss them, how much I long for them, and how badly I want them to come home. Even when that home feels broken by mortality. And yet, what I remember is not always that these were saints who love eternally. They were so much more than that, and it feels important to preserve their fullness. In preserving that fullness in this book, I hope to have humanized them and made them the real people they were to me and to those around us. And in writing about all the women I love, I hope to enshrine them.

To my Abuelita Cándida Rosa, I hope that you finally feel the fullness of the compassion you seldom gave to anyone because you weren't given it freely.

To my Prima Kati, from you I have seen a willingness to show up for people. From you I have witnessed the strength of believing you can always do more. You are invincible because of the way people show up for you in kind.

To my Tía Yesi, you are judged so cruelly, and yet out of all the women in our family you have stood loyal next to your husband and children. You have not let outside voices and opinions force you to treat your children any differently, and your loyalty taught me about the power we give to naysayers and how to do better. From you, I sample my I-don't-give-a-fuck attitude regularly.

To my Tía Carolina, you have always been in the background of my memories. Your husband overpowered any room you shared with him, and I do not remember your words but I remember your gestures. You were always quick to rub a shoulder when you discerned discomfort. You were always quick to open your home and cook food for people you love. Your home and your spirit transformed when that man was not around. You taught me that men can keep their limelight; we can create spaces for us that are in the shadows if it means that is where we can thrive.

To my Prima Lesbia, you were always my favorite person to share my life with; you understood me. I have seen you bend for those who expect you to have supernatural talents for carrying the expectations of others. But I also have seen you find ways to win, ways to get your way, ways of subverting situations for your benefit. You were told not to have needs, and instead you turned around and made them believe your needs were theirs in order to get what you needed. From you, I've taken a sample from a reservoir of genius.

To my Prima Ilse, your willingness to move past other people's shame to ensure that our family is okay is an example to others. No one has ever spoken a bad word about you, even when you gave them reason to do so, and that is a testament to your ingenuity and strength. With you, I draw from your fighting spirit.

To my mami, you are an exceptional teacher. You do not force people to treat you better or nicer; you make people see their mistakes by pure determination. You are no rogada, and the way you manage to hold your head high when everything around you is meant to kill your pride is magnificent. You are the first feminist icon I encountered, and I got to be raised by you. I am so fucking lucky. I am often told I am just like you, and I think of all the good things that means, from your insistence that you cook only what you want to eat to washing only your own dishes, doing only your own laundry, and your secret stash of money. I saw you constantly fight for yourself, and I channel that daily.

To my Prima Alba, you have surpassed yourself at every turn. When the world wants to put you in a box, you stretch yourself past it. You have taught me what it means to do life on your terms, what you lose and what you gain, and you have gained so much. Your freedom within yourself and your ability to live the life you designed for yourself is my goal in life. I want what you have, and you laid a path to get there for me to follow. You fucking did it, and I love that for us.

To my Prima Courtney, your cunning defiance has always entranced me. I feel so small next to you, but in the best ways. Like I get to witness someone so profoundly big and proud exist. I have an image of you carved in my head of your arms stretched to each side, standing barefoot in a grassy field, looking up to the sky with your eyes closed. You are velvet, smooth, soft, and beautiful.

To my Prima Raquel, you have lost so much and yet you kept going. You have shown me that grieving should not be hidden for the comfort of others. Who we harm when we hide our fullness is ourselves. Your prioritizing your time has been phenomenal to witness. I wish lightness for you this upcoming year.

To my Prima Johanna, we have been carving our friendship at a pace that has felt good to both of us. I have loved watching our friendship bloom over time. Watching you endure pain has been hard to witness, but your relentlessness and your ability to stay steady have shown me what it looks like to withstand pain and not turn toxic. We have options, and we can grow past bad habits. I am lucky I get to see your growth.

To my Prima Kristian, I cannot believe the past few years you have had. You amaze me at every turn and with every new obstacle you tackle so furiously. Sitting with you and discussing life, love, and those who drain us has kept me whole in moments I was seconds from extinguishing. Our friendship transcends the internet.

To my Abuelita Rosa Esperanza, I hope that you are resting in the afterlife. If God is a woman, she has your rough hands and soft touch. This book is all my dreams for us, all my love I could write down and manifest onto us. And yet, it only scratched the surface.

I wrote this book for my family, for my chosen sisters, for us, and for me. Las quiero mucho.

ACKNOWLEDGMENTS

My acknowledgments section here is to include those I did not mention in my conclusion. I want to take a moment to thank my two wonderful literary agents, Aemilia Phillips and David Patterson. Sometimes I think I am the most irritating person to work with, yet the two of them are quick to tell me I am the norm (ha ha!) and maybe even pleasant. Thank you for finding me on Twitter, David. I underestimated you, and here I am eating my words. Aemilia, I have always felt your unwavering belief in my art, and I am grateful you stick around and answer my every concern.

To Emma, my original editor at Seal for this book, thank you for fighting for this book and ensuring I got what I wanted. I shaped this book right before your very eyes. I can't believe it is finished. To Emily, my current editor for this book, thank you for your flexibility in meeting my needs. I have enjoyed our chats and continue to look forward to working together.

To my sister, who manages my work calendar, you are an angel. I would not be able to do half of what I do without your help. Thank you for making my life easier! And also just for always having my back since we were kids. I love you so much.

To my partner, it has been a joy to watch our friendship blossom. I think you are my first and only guy friend, and it has been an honor to have that friendship with someone I also love romantically. Thank you for accompanying me and cheering me on as I tackle new and exciting career opportunities. I can't wait to continue to live life alongside you.

To my reader, Kristian, thank you for your brilliance. I cannot believe your willingness to always help me figure out what I am trying to say and never back down from telling me what you think. I am honored to know you. You get two acknowledgments from me, and many more to come!

To Josie Del Castillo, I cannot believe I got my favorite artist to make these illustrations within this book. Thank you for your willingness and your realness. I have enjoyed getting to know you and cooking for you.

To the person who discovered me years back when I was writing long captions on Instagram and calling it a "rant," Tanisha Love Ramirez. You always believed I was a writer even when I did not see it. I cannot believe I get to do this for a living, and you did that! You opened doors for me, and my entire life changed. I will never forget it.

To everyone I inevitably forgot, because I always leave this part till the end due to how it overwhelms me, thank you for supporting me in the many ways so many of you do. And thank you for cheering me on and buying my books.

NOTES

There are three books I would refer to as my primary sources that I used to contextualize my lived experiences with my family and chosen family. I read seventy sources for this book, but two in particular were used heavily throughout. As I read feminist takes on archetypes, I found Clarissa Pinkola Estés and Simone de Beauvoir to have the most work to expand on through my own body of knowledge. Pinkola Estés's *Women Who Run with the Wolves* was a book that was recommended to me in 2013, and I have read and reread it throughout various stages in my life. The way that Pinkola Estés breaks down traditional nursery rhymes and bedtime stories to explore female archetypes gave me foundational stepping stones in going about the deconstruction of my own archetypes. Similarly, de Beauvoir's *The Second Sex* offered a plethora of knowledge to build from and examine through my non-white lens. I recommend my readers dive into these books if they are interested in female archetypes.

Not all the texts I used as research are mentioned in my notes for each chapter. Instead, I am highlighting the prominent voices and quotes I utilized in the specific chapters. Look to my bibliography for more detailed reads.

Chapter 1: La Matriarch

The matriarch chapter is about the toll of female labor. In terms of my sources, I used a lot of books to situate my reading of this archetype. Cherríe Moraga is a matriarch of her own—motherless but a foremother of Latina queer feminists—and so I utilized various texts of hers, which can all be found in my bibliography.

Simone de Beauvoir's *Second Sex* has an entire section on the grandmother and the aging woman, which helped support some of my first-person encounters with matriarchs in relation to their husbands. *The Will to Change: Men, Masculinity, and Love* by bell hooks was instrumental as she has some of the more realistic takes on marriage and womanhood. I utilized her quotes from that book throughout the text.

Chapter 2: The Young Tía

Simone de Beauvoir's *The Second Sex* analysis on childhood and what she refers to as "the girl" gave me a lot to jump off from and a deeper reflection on my relationship to the young tía to bring those concepts into real life. I specifically wanted a deeper analysis of the stage between girlhood and womanhood, the sort-of initiation, and how that would feel to the tía and to those younger eyes spectating her.

My parents were an instrumental source for remembering some stories about this tía. And then I fused a bit from other young tías who are my contemporaries when it comes to the freedom a young tía embodies.

Chapter 3: La Prima Perfecta

Ultimately, childism is my principal topic of concern surrounding this archetype. A primary source was Elisabeth Young-Bruehl's *Childism: Confronting Prejudice Against Children.* This gave me the language around goodness and perfectionism for children in general, as well as unprocessed parent trauma. And then in terms of gendered perfectionism through girl-rearing, I relied on Sharon Lamb's *The Secret Lives of Girls: What Good Girls Really Do—Sex*

Play, Aggression, and Their Guilt. This entire book gave me a lot to work with in terms of differentiating childism from girl-rearing childism practices, which have long been documented by various feminist academics.

The good girl archetype is what the perfect prima is trying to unravel. Clarissa Pinkola Estés writes at length about this archetype, but seeing this archetype incarnated as my cousin and even myself gives it all a face and an experience that I think is needed when we talk about this type of parenting.

Finally, a source that I read when I was much younger to give me the perspective I needed to eventually write this chapter down is a study done by Julie Bettie documented in her book *Women Without Class: Girls, Race, and Identity.* To understand a good girl, you need to understand the construction of a bad girl and how Latina bodies are often seen as deviant. Compliance is a form of self-preservation within the status quo. This all helped me not vilify the good girl, but look toward the world around her.

Chapter 4: Widowed Tía

I knew that I wanted this chapter to show something that is glaringly obvious but unspoken, which is not grief upon the death of a husband, but rather relief. That is not to say that some people are not in love and truly heartbroken when their significant other dies. That is not the point; the point is sexism and the ways it manifests itself in heterosexual romantic relationships. The burden of being a woman in a heterosexual marriage should not be silenced for the male ego, and yet it happens.

When I was looking for sources, Simone de Beauvoir's *The Second Sex* was a primary one. But I also utilized bell hooks's *The Will to Change: Men, Masculinity, and Love* to a large extent because that book outlines a lot about the repression and violence that occur in intimate heterosexual dynamics.

Chapter 5: Tu Tía, la Loca

This archetype relies heavily on the research by Justin Charlebois titled *Gender and the Construction of Dominant, Hegemonic, and Oppositional Femininities.* I utilized his term "oppositional femininities" to give structure to the ideas behind this particular archetype. But I also read the essay by Sandra Lee Bartky titled "Foucault, Femininity, and the Modernization of Patriarchal Power" found in *The Politics of Women's Bodies: Sexuality, Appearance, and Behavior,* edited by Samantha Kwan and Rose Weitz, to help me name what is at stake for this type of defiant gender performance.

So much of this tía loca is also based on my own lived experiences as someone who is very much oppositional to my parents' rearing of me as a little girl. And so much of the angst around this is in meeting other women who have embodied defiance by doing nothing particularly deviant, but most definitely nothing traditional either.

Chapter 6: The Tía Who Sees Fantasmas

Early on, I was really aware of the fact that while this archetype was crucial to include, I did not want to limit her or ascribe anything to her. I wanted to leave more questions than answers when writing about this archetype, and Avery F. Gordon's *Ghostly Matters: Haunting and the Sociological Imagination* felt like a good source to shoulder that responsibility. Gordon's book does a great job at enumerating the endless possibilities for hauntings and ghost encounters. Gordon is also phenomenal at clarifying how words are not enough, and that in this particular conversation we cannot be restricted to the words available to us to make sense of the unexplainable.

Laura E. Pérez's *Chicana Art: The Politics of Spiritual and Aesthetic Altarities* is a staple in terms of trying to decolonize the spirituality of Latinas in particular, but also of women of color in general. I utilized Pérez's writings to center myself when I was trying to make sense of this archetype. A decolonial lens is highly important for these types of conversations, as well as necessary for my own writing process as I attempt to give this archetype some of her intelligence back since linear logical thinking will rob her of it. The quote within the chapter that comes from Ana Castillo is from Pérez's research and book.

Finally, Molefi Kete Asante's *The Afrocentric Idea* helped free me from the need to think of logic as one-dimensional. By introducing the term "afro-circular" to challenge European logic, it gave me the groundwork to take the power away from logic as European and expand on it. Europeans are not more logical; rather, they think in a linear logic while other communities in the Global South think with a different logic—a circular logic that is not confined to whiteness. This text helped me frame my argument away from whiteness.

Chapter 7: Street-Smart Prima

The level of allowable competence for women in particular class settings really depends on their level of commitment to preexisting value systems for women in general. Karin A. Martin's essay titled "Becoming a Gendered Body" found in the anthology *The Politics of Women's Bodies: Sexuality, Appearance, and Behavior*, edited by Samantha Kwan and Rose Weitz, provided me with the source necessary to contextualize the forces at play for a street-smart daughter/prima/woman. The ability to hear all that framing around proper womanhood, and somehow find a way to outsmart it, is unbelievable, especially at the level that a street-smart prima is operating within. This chapter was really about trying to fully describe her cleverness while contrasting it with sources that heavily touch on the complex, systemic levels of socialization surrounding girl-rearing.

Julie Bettie's book *Women Without Class: Girls, Race, and Identity* gives me a lot of necessary information to fully understand the intersection of race, class, and gender. The forces working against this archetype are many, and those three are just the tip of the iceberg.

Chapter 8: Dignified Tía

I struggled with what to name this tía, and then one of my friends who is a professor and does a lot of Latina theory and theorizing, Dr. Maria Chavez, dropped the term "dignified" on my lap as I was describing this chapter, and it felt perfect.

When writing about her, I realized how the dignified tía is a matriarch and the perfect prima is a pipeline to her. They fight the same demons, so the same sources were useful for these three sections. I used the reliable Sharon Lamb's *The Secret Lives of Girls: What Good Girls Really Do—Sex Play, Aggression, and Their Guilt* since it was such an instrumental reference for the perfect prima. I also used Simone de Beauvoir's *The Second Sex*, specifically the motherhood section, to paint this archetype within my perspective as a daughter formed under the watchful eye of a dignified woman. And of course, I used Clarissa Pinkola Estés's *Women Who Run with the Wolves* since these three archetypes (perfect prima, dignified tía, matriarch) are foundational to my book as much as these sources.

Chapter 9: Tía Who Loves Plants and Animals

The secondary status of being a woman stems from thinking women are more bodily, and I knew that was an important element to this book because men do not lack bodies but are told they are superior for this ability to be headier and more logical. What would it mean to elevate bodies to the same playing field instead of imposing these hierarchies in which they told us one was beneath the other?

A great source for this was Naomi R. Goldenberg's *Resurrecting the Body: Feminism, Religion, and Psychoanalysis*. I write about this book being an incarnation of memories, and animating and recalling memories into flesh feels particularly important for my creative process. In that vein, I wanted to elevate that entire premise through Goldenberg's writings.

Chapter 10: Tu Tía Escandalosa

The primary text for this chapter is Jillian Hernandez's *Aesthetics of Excess: The Art and Politics of Black and Latina Embodiment*. I have waited almost a decade for this book to come out after reading an essay of Hernandez's years ago while in graduate school. The way she describes chongas and chusma, and her overall analysis of race and gender and class, was instrumental in giving this archetype shape and form.

Understanding that Latinas are read in a particular way by the white gaze, and that they are also read in particular ways within our communities, means understanding social control. Finding the words for this archetype was easy given Hernandez's support through her writings.

Chapter 11: Prima Who Doesn't Like Other Women

A primary text for this prima is Bonnie Burstow's *Radical Feminist Therapy: Working in the Context of Violence*. I often start my books with research first, and then I allow the research to shape where the book is heading. And this chapter felt so clear once I read that text. I was itching to write this chapter after reading Burstow's take on the insidious nature surrounding girlhood and the male gaze.

Chapter 12: The Childless Tía

A primary text for this particular chapter was Naomi Goldenberg's *Resurrecting the Body: Feminism, Religion, and Psychoanalysis*. So much of the burden of a childless woman is in the assumptions made about her body and her anatomy. This source helped frame a lot of that and root the solution in viewing this particular archetype as a person and not a vessel. This book was also a useful tool for working through archetypes by reading a feminist text that attempts to expand on Jung's archetypes.

Again, de Beauvoir's *The Second Sex* analysis on the mother archetype was useful in deconstructing the pipeline from womanhood to motherhood.

Chapter 13: The "Te Estás Engordando" Tía

I had a few texts that I relied on heavily for this chapter, but a foundational text here was Sabrina Strings's *Fearing the Black Body: The Racial Origins of Fat Phobia*. My disgust for fatphobia is rooted in understanding its anti-Black history.

I write about the diet panopticon based on the concept of panopticon from Michel Foucault's *Discipline and Punish*. This ever-present surveillance felt relevant to this chapter about diet culture.

I knew I wanted a fat writer to serve as the backbone of this chapter, and Aubrey Gordon's new book *"You Just Need to Lose Weight": And 19 Other Myths About Fat People* was instrumental. Aubrey also has a wonderful podcast where she tackles popular diets and the myth of the body mass index. I believe it is important to center fat activists for the body of knowledge they are producing. I hope this book leads you to many new discoveries. I encourage you to read and follow Latina fat activist Virgie Tovar, poet Yesika Salgado, and non-binary Latine author Caleb Luna.

Chapter 14: Book-Smart Prima

I attended the Latina Roundtable, a Latinas in philosophy conference hosted annually by a Nicaraguan scholar in philosophy named Dr. Mariana Ortega at Marquette University in Milwaukee, Wisconsin. This year's scholar of note was Maria Lugones, and I was introduced to the term "world traveler" as a means of describing someone who can walk between different contexts not by disrupting or centering herself, but as an act of deep connection.

That is the primary text of this chapter: *Pilgrimages/Peregrinajes: Theorizing Coalition Against Multiple Oppressions* by Lugones. Cherríe Moraga is the first of firsts, in my book, so her work is found throughout my book and especially in this chapter. I have cited all of the books I used of hers in my bibliography.

I used several articles from the anthology *Presumed Incompetent: The Intersections of Race and Class for Women in Academia*, edited by Gabriella Gutiérrez y Muhs et al., including Stephanie Shields's essay "Waking Up to Privilege: Intersectionality and Opportunity." Shields's essay does a lot to unpack the disproportionate class differences within academic spaces. The introduction from Angela Harris and Carmen Gonzalez was illustrative in the ways that women of color face particular obstacles their white male counterparts do not. Linda Trinh Vo's essay "Navigating the Academic Terrain: The Racial and Gender Politics of Elusive Belonging" provided instrumental research for the disparities experienced by women of color in academia.

Finally, Kimberlé Crenshaw is the originator of the term "intersectional feminism," and whenever I am thinking about intersections, I run to her. The quote I used for this chapter is from an anthology edited by Crenshaw titled *Critical Race Theory: The Key Writings that Formed the Movement*.

Chapter 15: Divorced Tía

In terms of a primary text for this chapter, I relied heavily on Emily Joy Allison's book *#ChurchToo: How Purity Culture Upholds Abuse and How to Find Healing*. Allison is one of the originators of the #ChurchToo movement. I quote her generously throughout the book, as purity culture is oftentimes the lens we use to judge the divorced tía.

Pinkola Estés's *Women Who Run with the Wolves* rears its head whenever I am attempting to critique systems that support a patriarchal society, which this chapter attempts to do.

Chapter 16: Second Mom Tía

For this chapter I primarily relied on Bonnie Burstow's *Radical Feminist Therapy: Working in the Context of Violence* to build my argument for female friendships. If you understand the violence of the patriarchy and how it impacts the formation of women in a general sense, you will understand how separating women into heterosexual households is complicit in the patriarchy. Burstow has an entire section on separating women and the harm this does, which was instrumental.

I also relied on Cherríe Moraga's poetry. She has a lot of wonderful and dense material around female friendships and her mother, which helped me give the chapter some wings.

Chapter 17: WhatsApp Tía

When I first conceptualized writing about this tía, who in my bones felt so real, I struggled with finding sources that talked about the obvious intersection of Latine immigrants and WhatsApp. Maybe it is so obvious that it need not be spoken or written about, or maybe my limits of being someone outside academia mean I just failed to access the correct journal. Either way, I did find an article that discussed the significance of WhatsApp and social media, but it was in South Indian culture written by Shriram Venkatraman at the UCL Press titled "Relationships: Kinship on Social Media." And it was extraordinary. Everything I was thinking, everything I understand about communication through cell phones and social media, was examined, and through that lens I found a source from which I could draw plenty of similarities despite the geographic differences.

Chapter 18: La Tía Cuir

I have been wanting to write this chapter for a really long time. As a queer Latina raised in a Christian household, I find my story in hushed corners of empty rooms and never in books. So I wrote what I needed to see written. My primary source for this chapter is Katie L. Acosta's *Amigas y Amantes: Sexually Nonconforming Latinas Negotiate Family.* I love Acosta's take on this topic, and I wish there were more like this.

Chapter 19: MLM Tía

I knew this tía was sitting on the doorstep of further deconstructing the myth of meritocracy. There is an abundance of takes on MLMs, and I read a few journal articles about it all, but ultimately my position about meritocracy is fully informed by David K. Shipler's *The Working Poor: Invisible in America.*

I also cited and relied on an anthropological study done on a Mexican population's relationship to MLMs written by Peter S. Cahn and titled "Consuming Class: Multilevel Marketers in Neoliberal Mexico." And an essay by Janny Scott found in *Class Matters* titled "Life at the Top in America Isn't Just Better, It's Longer." This article supported my argument around the illusiveness of class mobility, immigrants and their work ethics, and the negative effects on immigrants' health.

Chapter 20: Your "Pretty" Prima

When I first wrote this chapter, I focused heavily on colorism as the sole topic to unpack. But the more I researched for the book and read more and more about femininity and heteronormativity, and the ways we raise girls to be pretty because they will earn a husband, it became so much more.

I was keen on unpacking the race aspect of it all by looking at C. Wright Mills's *The Racial Contract.* Writing from a non-Black perspective, I wanted to talk about how prettiness and beauty are tools of a racist society.

But then I also understood through my research that whiteness, femininity, and heteronormativity go hand in hand via my readings of people like Sharon Lamb in *The Secret Lives of Girls: What Good Girls Really Do—Sex Play, Aggression, and Their Guilt.* And removing the blame from particular people is important when talking about systemic issues like sexism and raising girls, so Justin Charlebois's *Gender and the Construction of Dominant, Hegemonic, and Oppositional Femininities* is often quoted in a lot of texts discussing traditional femininity. Finally, Sandra Lee Bartky's essay "Foucault, Femininity, and the Modernization of Patriarchal Power" gave me the perfect words to finally get this chapter to sound like I needed it to sound. Her analysis on femininity and the patriarchy was instrumental in getting this archetype to have a well-rounded analysis.

BIBLIOGRAPHY

Aborn, Shana. 2022. "Is Mary Kay an MLM?" *The List*. January 31. https://www.thelist.com/752047/is-mary-kay-an-mlm/.

Acosta, Katie L. 2013. *Amigas y Amantes: Sexually Nonconforming Latinas Negotiate Family*. Families in Focus. New Brunswick: Rutgers University Press.

Allison, Emily Joy. 2021. *#ChurchToo: How Purity Culture Upholds Abuse and How to Find Healing*. Minneapolis: Broadleaf Books.

Anzaldúa, Gloria, and AnaLouise Keating. 2015. *Light in the Dark: Luz en lo Oscuro: Rewriting Identity, Spirituality, Reality*. Latin America Otherwise: Languages, Empires, Nations. Durham: Duke University Press.

Beauvoir, Simone de, Constance Capisto-Borde, and Sheila Malovany-Chevallier. 2011. *The Second Sex*. First Vintage Books ed. New York: Vintage Books.

BetterGoods.org. 2022. "The Controversy Behind Popular MLM Hair Care Brand Monat." March 19. https://bettergoods.org/monat/.

Bettie, Julie. 2014. *Women Without Class: Girls, Race, and Identity; with a New Introduction*. Oakland: University of California Press.

Burstow, Bonnie. 1992. *Radical Feminist Therapy: Working in the Context of Violence*. Newbury Park: Sage Publications.

Bushnell, Mona. n.d. "Are MLMs Scams or Entrepreneurial Opportunities?" Business.com. Accessed October 1, 2023. https://www.business.com/articles/mlms-target-women-and-immigrants/.

Butler, Judith. 2011. *Bodies That Matter: On the Discursive Limits of Sex*. Routledge Classics. New York: Routledge.

Cahn, Peter S. 2008. "Consuming Class: Multilevel Marketers in Neoliberal Mexico." *Cultural Anthropology* 23 (3): 429–52.

Cain, Sian. 2019. "Women Are Happier Without Children or a Spouse, Says Happiness Expert." *The Observer*, sec. Life and Style. May 25. https://www.theguardian.com/lifeandstyle/2019/may/25/women-happier-without-children-or-a-spouse-happiness-expert.

Carruthers, Charlene A. 2018. *Unapologetic: A Black, Queer, and Feminist Mandate for Radical Movements*. Boston: Beacon Press.

Castillo, Ana, ed. 1996. *Goddess of the Americas: La Diosa de las Américas: Writings on the Virgin of Guadalupe*. New York: Riverhead Books.

Charlebois, Justin. 2011. *Gender and the Construction of Dominant, Hegemonic, and Oppositional Femininities*. Lanham: Lexington Books.

Cheng, Anne Anlin. 2013. *Second Skin: Josephine Baker and the Modern Surface*. Paperback ed. New York: Oxford University Press.

Class Matters. 2005. 1st ed. New York: Times Books.

Cleage, Pearl. 1994. *Deals with the Devil, and Other Reasons to Riot*. First Ballantine Books trade paperback ed. New York: Ballantine.

———. 2014. *Things I Should Have Told My Daughter: Lies, Lessons & Love Affairs*. First Atria Books hardcover ed. New York: Atria Books.

Cohen, Cathy J. 2004. "DEVIANCE AS RESISTANCE: A New Research Agenda for the Study of Black Politics." *Du Bois Review: Social Science Research on Race* 1 (1): 27–45. https://doi.org/10.1017/S1742058X04040044.

Crenshaw, Kimberlé, ed. 1995. *Critical Race Theory: The Key Writings That Formed the Movement*. New York: New Press.

Cypess, Sandra Messinger. 1991. *La Malinche in Mexican Literature from History to Myth*. First ed. The Texas Pan American Series. Austin: University of Texas Press.

Del Castillo, Adelaida R., ed. 2005. *Between Borders: Essays on Mexicana/Chicana History*. La Mujer Latina Series. Mountain View: Floricanto Press.

Estés, Clarissa Pinkola. 1997. *Women Who Run with the Wolves: Myths and Stories of the Wild Woman Archetype*. Repr. Ballantine Books. New York: Ballantine Books.

Fischer-Mirkin, Toby. 1995. *Dress Code: Understanding the Hidden Meanings of Women's Clothes*. First ed. New York: Clarkson Potter.

Freeman, Margaret L. 2020. *Women of Discriminating Taste: White Sororities and the Making of American Ladyhood*. Athens: University of Georgia Press.

Freire, Paulo, Donaldo P. Macedo, and Ira Shor. 2018. *Pedagogy of the Oppressed*. Translated by Myra Bergman Ramos. Fiftieth anniversary ed. New York: Bloomsbury Academic.

Gill, Tiffany M. 2010. *Beauty Shop Politics: African American Women's Activism in the Beauty Industry*. Women in American History. Champaign: University of Illinois Press.

Glisch-Sánchez, David Luis, and Nic Rodríguez-Villafañe, eds. 2023. *Sana, Sana: Latinx Pain and Radical Visions for Healing and Justice*. Philadelphia: Common Notions.

Goldenberg, Naomi R. 1993. *Resurrecting the Body: Feminism, Religion, and Psychotherapy*. New York: Crossroad.

Gomez, Edgar. 2022. *High-Risk Homosexual: A Memoir*. New York: Soft Skull.

González, Juan. 2011. *Harvest of Empire: A History of Latinos in America*. Revised ed. New York: Penguin Books.

González, Rigoberto. 2011. *Butterfly Boy: Memories of a Chicano Mariposa*. Madison: University of Wisconsin Press.

Gordon, Avery. 2008. *Ghostly Matters: Haunting and the Sociological Imagination*. Minneapolis: University of Minnesota Press.

———. 2023. *"You Just Need to Lose Weight": And 19 Other Myths About Fat People*. Boston: Beacon Press.

Grayson, Kent. 2007. "Friendship Versus Business in Marketing Relationships." *Journal of Marketing* 71 (4): 121–39.

Gutiérrez y Muhs, Gabriella, et al., ed. 2012. *Presumed Incompetent: The Intersections of Race and Class for Women in Academia*. Boulder: University Press of Colorado.

Hall, Stuart, Jessica Evans, and Sean Nixon, eds. 2013. *Representation*. Second ed. Milton Keynes, United Kingdom: The Open University Press.

Harris, Angela P., and Carmen G. Gonzalez. 2012. Introduction to *Presumed Incompetent: The Intersections of Race and Class for Women in Academia*. Edited by Gabriella Gutiérrez y Muhs et al. Boulder: University Press of Colorado, 1–16.

Hernandez, Jillian. 2020. *Aesthetics of Excess: The Art and Politics of Black and Latina Embodiment*. Durham: Duke University Press.

Hill Collins, Patricia. 2004. *Black Sexual Politics: African Americans, Gender, and the New Racism*. New York: Routledge.

Hill, Susan E. 2011. *Eating to Excess: The Meaning of Gluttony and the Fat Body in the Ancient World*. Praeger Series on the Ancient World. Santa Barbara: Praeger.

Kang, Miliann. 2010. *The Managed Hand: Race, Gender, and the Body in Beauty Service Work*. Berkeley: University of California Press.

Kapadia, Ronak K. 2019. *Insurgent Aesthetics: Security and the Queer Life of the Forever War*. Art History Publication Initiative. Durham: Duke University Press.

Lagarde y de los Rios, Marcela. 2014. *Los cautiverios de las Mujeres: madresposas, monjas, putas, presas y locas*. Ciudad de México: Siglo Veintiuno Editores.

Lamb, Sharon. 2001. *The Secret Lives of Girls: What Good Girls Really Do—Sex Play, Aggression, and Their Guilt*. New York: Free Press.

Levin-Epstein, Amy. 2012. "Is Mary Kay a 'Pink Pyramid' Scheme?— CBS News." August 23. https://www.cbsnews.com/news/is -mary-kay-a-pink-pyramid-scheme/.

Lugones, Maria. 2003. *Pilgrimages/Peregrinajes: Theorizing Coalition Against Multiple Oppressions*. Feminist Constructions. Lanham: Rowman & Littlefield.

Mendible, Myra, ed. 2007. *From Bananas to Buttocks: The Latina Body in Popular Film and Culture*. First ed. Austin: University of Texas Press.

Mills, Charles W. 2011. *The Racial Contract*. Ithaca: Cornell University Press.

Mitchell, Elizabeth S. 2022. "Is Monat an MLM?" *The List*. January 31. https://www.thelist.com/752202/is-monat-an-mlm/.

Mora, Lauren. n.d. "Hispanic Enrollment Reaches New High at Four-Year Colleges in the U.S., but Affordability Remains an Obstacle." *Pew Research Center* (blog). Accessed November 13, 2023. https://www.pewresearch.org/short-reads/2022/10/07/hispanic -enrollment-reaches-new-high-at-four-year-colleges-in-the -u-s-but-affordability-remains-an-obstacle/.

Moraga, Cherríe. 1983. *Loving in the War Years: Lo Que Nunca Pasó Por Sus Labios*. Boston: South End Press.

Moraga, Cherríe, and Gloria Anzaldúa, eds. 2015. *This Bridge Called My Back: Writings by Radical Women of Color*. Fourth ed. Albany: State University of New York (SUNY) Press.

Muñoz, José Esteban. 1999. *Disidentifications: Queers of Color and the Performance of Politics*. Cultural Studies of the Americas, v. 2. Minneapolis: University of Minnesota Press.

O'Keefe, R. B., and J. E. Kinsella. 1979. "Alkaline Phosphatase from Bovine Mammary Tissue: Purification and Some Molecular and

Catalytic Properties." *International Journal of Biochemistry* 10 (2): 125–34. https://doi.org/10.1016/0020-711x(79)90107-1.

Pérez, Laura Elisa. 2007. *Chicana Art: The Politics of Spiritual and Aesthetic Altarities.* Objects/Histories. Durham: Duke University Press.

Projansky, Sarah. 2014. *Spectacular Girls: Media Fascination and Celebrity Culture.* New York: New York University Press.

Quinney, Richard. 1980. *Class, State, & Crime.* Second ed. New York: Longman.

Romero, Rolando, and Amanda Nolacea Harris, eds. 2005. *Feminism, Nation and Myth: La Malinche.* Houston: Arte Público Press.

Salamon, Gayle. 2010. *Assuming a Body: Transgender and Rhetorics of Materiality.* New York: Columbia University Press.

Shields, Stephanie A. 2012. "Waking Up to Privilege: Intersectionality and Opportunity." In *Presumed Incompetent: The Intersections of Race and Class for Women in Academia.* Edited by Gabriella Gutiérrez y Muhs et al. Boulder: University Press of Colorado, 29–39.

Shipler, David K. 2005. *The Working Poor: Invisible in America.* First Vintage Books ed. New York: Vintage Books.

Shire, Warsan. 2022. *Bless the Daughter Raised by a Voice in Her Head.* London: Chatto & Windus.

Soto, Lilia. 2018. *Girlhood in the Borderlands: Mexican Teens Caught in the Crossroads of Migration.* New York: New York University Press.

Strings, Sabrina. 2019. *Fearing the Black Body: The Racial Origins of Fat Phobia.* New York: New York University Press.

Trinh Vo, Linda. 2012. "Navigating the Academic Terrain: The Racial and Gender Politics of Elusive Belonging." In *Presumed Incompetent: The Intersections of Race and Class for Women in Academia.* Edited by Gabriella Gutiérrez y Muhs et al. Boulder: University Press of Colorado, 93–112.

Troyano, Alina, Ela Troyano, Uzi Parnes, and Chon A. Noriega. 2000. *I, Carmelita Tropicana: Performing Between Cultures*. Boston: Beacon Press.

Venkatraman, Shriram. 2017. "Relationships: Kinship on Social Media." In *Social Media in South India*, 101–35. UCL Press. https://doi.org/10.2307/j.ctt1qnw88r.10.

Walker, Alice. 2006. *We Are the Ones We Have Been Waiting For: Inner Light in a Time of Darkness: Meditations*. New York: New Press. Distributed by W. W. Norton.

———. 2010. *Hard Times Require Furious Dancing: New Poems*. Novato: New World Library.

Weheliye, Alexander G. 2014. *Habeas Viscus: Racializing Assemblages, Biopolitics, and Black Feminist Theories of the Human*. Durham: Duke University Press.

Weitz, Rose, and Samantha Kwan, eds. 2014. *The Politics of Women's Bodies: Sexuality, Appearance, and Behavior*. Fourth ed. Oxford: Oxford University Press.

Young-Bruehl, Elisabeth. 2012. *Childism: Confronting Prejudice Against Children*. New Haven: Yale University Press.

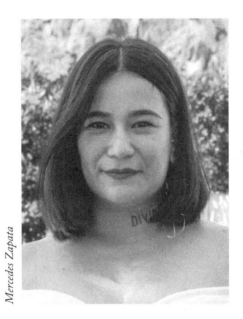

Mercedes Zapata

Prisca Dorcas Mojica Rodríguez is a leading Latine activist, writer, and speaker. She is the founder of Latina Rebels, a platform with over 350,000 followers, and the author of *For Brown Girls with Sharp Edges and Tender Hearts*. Her work has been featured on NPR, and in *New York Magazine*'s The Cut, *Teen Vogue*, and *Cosmopolitan*. She earned her master of divinity from Vanderbilt University and lives in Nashville, Tennessee.